To my parents.

Miss Expatria

Prologue

7 October 2003

A year ago today, I started this life.

A year ago today, friends came to my aid: Katie retrieved me from Cynthia's house, where I had holed up after breaking off a passionate but ultimately impossible seven-year relationship with my boyfriend, Pavlov Memento, on the advice of a Jesus-loving taxi driver while on the New Jersey Turnpike.

Pavlov Memento got his name from another friend, Rienzo, who once described him as someone who, if he were one of Pavlov's dogs, would consistently wonder why the bell was ringing and then be surprised and thrilled when the meat arrived; Rienzo also likened him to the main character in Memento, as his inability to connect people, events, or even sentences to each other must have been due to a complete lapse in short term memory.

I was due to leave the country in two days, to start a new life with him in Rome. Now, I was about to do it alone.

Katie and I went to Avenue C to deposit dear sweet Lillian Cat at her new home. This was something Pavlov Memento was supposed to have taken care of, but of course he never followed through.

Miss Expatria

Next stop was the bank, where I took out half of our savings to give to Pavlov Memento. Somehow, this made the breakup seem more real. I was shaking and Katie was hugging me and we were both freaking out at the enormity of the situation, while the teller tried to decide whether we were an elaborate distraction for a heist.

The travel agent called at some point that morning and told me to go to the Empire State Building to retrieve my new, one-way ticket to my new life. I was terrified of being on the same plane with Pavlov Memento; he had become unpredictable. I changed my ticket to escape being in a confined area for nine hours with that unpredictability. Only fitting that my final day in New York included a stop at its last standing famous skyscraper.

We spent a fortune on numerous taxis for all of these errands, in order to avoid pulic displays of broken-upedness. We made it back to Katie's place and I repacked what I had thrown into an overnight bag in my rush to avoid another moment in the apartment I shared with Pavlov. We screamed along to Mary J. Blige's "No More Drama" and reminded each other to breathe and burst into laughter at the fact that my life had just taken a hard right turn.

There were phone calls to other friends - Mary Kate, Jackie, Howie; a message left for Dana that changed so much; numerous favors asked of so many people. I had never asked anything of anyone, ever; it is not in my nature. But this time I asked, and every single one of them delivered, no questions, with nothing but love and supportive words for me. I owe Cynthia, Katie, Jackie and

Mary Kate more than I could ever possibly give them. I literally could not have done what I did without these women at my side.

The car service arrived, courtesy of a print vendor from work. I hugged Katie, and we laughed and cried at the same time, and I got in the car and left, leaving her the money and my cell phone; she agreed to wait for Pavlov Memento to call and give it all to him - and to keep my early departure a secret.

I got on the plane, popped a Valium, and cried. I did it. I did it. I did it. I did it. It was the only phrase I could fit into a head crammed with thoughts and images from the past, and hopes and fears for the future.

I remembered when I was in therapy after 9/11 to get a handle on some recurring nightmares I was having. I told Dr. Cohen that usually, when I am about to start any large project or adventure, I have a clear picture of the final result in my head – but that when I thought about moving to Rome, it was blank.

She told me it was because I had no frame of reference for what I was about to do, but I knew it was something else. If you had asked me then what I thought it might be, I would never in a million years have said it was that I would end the longest, most defining relationship I had ever had. But when I did end it, the images came flooding in – and I knew I had done what I needed to do.

And now here I am, one year later. How can I ever properly describe this last year of my life? How can I possibly put into words how I became the person I discovered I have always been?

I love myself. I love my life.

He pushed me, and I flew.

Chapter One

The plane landed at Fiumicino. Seeing the stone pines and the sea, and hearing the Italians applaud a good landing, I cried again – this time, with overwhelming joy and relief. I really had done it.

A family friend I had never met before with the improbable name of Hank Decker picked me up from the airport and took me to his home in Lavinio, on the Mediterranean coast, about an hour from Rome. He lived with a tiny, bird-like woman named Chiara and her teenage son Federico, and he clearly had no idea what to do with either of them.

Hank was a retired cop from the States and during the 20-minute ride to his home, I discovered he loved Nixon, hated black people, was thinking about going vigilante on the Taliban, and wished he were living in Malaysia. I was emotionally drained, jetlagged, and a passenger in a tiny Fiat that was hurtling at ungodly speeds down an unpaved road, so I decided not to provoke an argument with the only person I knew in Italy.

He was a strange character, but there is no one I would have rather had in the house than a racist ex-cop itching for action when Pavlov Memento showed up the next day.

It was the message I left for my friend of 20 years, Dana. I was purposely vague, but I guess the panic came through in my voice; when she couldn't get a hold of me she called Pavlov, who had my cell phone and told her his version of what had happened. She encouraged him to fly over and win me back.

We heard the taxi pull up as we were having breakfast, and though Hank said he was expecting a package, I knew it was Pavlov. I started shaking. I had no idea what kind of mood he would be in, and I was scared – but whatever his intentions might have been, died immediately upon his noticing the size and demeanor of the man blocking the path to the house.

"Hi, my name is – "

"I know who you are. Are you going to cause any trouble here?"

Pavlov looked past him and saw me cowering in the doorway. "No, I've just come to talk to Christine."

"OK, you can come in. But you try anything and I'll have your ass on the next plane back to the States. Understand?"

"Yessir."

My new hero let us have some privacy in his downstairs living room. We sat in matching armchairs, facing each other, like heads of state from warring nations. I had nothing to say; he had crossed a line and there was no taking it back.

Miss Expatria

The exact conversation we had is not important. The crux of it was that he thought I had ended our seven-year relationship because he would not drive me to my family's house three days prior. Neither my dramatic exit from the country, nor any one of the hundreds of dire warnings I had given him in the last year, had given him the tip-off that maybe things would not turn out so well.

After hearing his bumbling, ignorant, pathetic excuses I told him once again that it was over, and I offered to have Hank drive him to wherever he'd like to stay. We took a shell-shocked Pavlov to a hotel in Anzio, the next town over – the one we lived in for a while after 9/11, which is another whole story - and as we pulled away, leaving him bewildered and starting to cry, Hank asked me if I was alright.

"Never felt better. Can we go to that market you were telling me about? I need stuff for my new place."

Chapter Two

Hank and Chiara had shown me three places in Lavinio to choose from that first afternoon I arrived. After we had seen the first two, I started to panic quietly about living in this tiny, isolated town so far from Rome.

Then we saw the third place. It was the entire top floor of a large, rambling palazzo two houses from the beach. As we walked from room to room, Chiara opened the shutters to reveal a spectacular view of the sparkling, placid Mediterranean under an endless blue sky.

"I'll take this one."

§

Let me just say this:

If you ever break up with someone, leave the country and live alone by the sea for a few months.

Everything was so utterly, literally foreign to me that I had no choice but to move relentlessly ahead with my life and concentrate on myself, purely to survive.

Miss Expatria

I worked on my Italian. I destroyed local cuisine with my cooking experiments. I watched movies on my laptop. I filled an entire notebook with everything I ever wanted to say to Pavlov Memento. I cried, sometimes. I built ever-more elaborate tinfoil mobiles to keep the pigeons off the back balcony. I learned how to use Italian appliances and how to shop at Italian markets.

But most importantly, I learned who I was and what I was capable of. And I never looked back.

§

Every Wednesday is Lavinio's market day. Several streets are blocked off to allow for a long line of vendors selling everything you could ever want, in no particularly organized fashion – kitchen utensils, jeans, fruit, vegetables, lingerie, down comforters, shoes, meat, clock radios, cheese, flowers, CDs, purses in haphazard piles.

Every Tuesday night I would sit down with my translation dictionary and make a list of the things I needed, in case I needed to talk about them when I got there. But for the most part, the good thing about shopping this way was that I did not have to speak too often. I would gather up my purchases, show them to the vendor, and pay without saying more than *buon giorno* or *grazie*. I did not want to be outed as The American. I desperately wanted to fit in, which unfortunately often robbed me of the ability to speak at all.

Miss Expatria

But my deep and abiding love for all things dairy finally forced me to reveal my gulping, stuttering self to the Cheese Lady.

She was probably about 50; she was built like a Parma ham and had hands like baseball mitts. Her warm, genuine smile and the intoxicating smells from her stall targeted her as My First Italian.

Oh, how I studied the night before. I wanted to make sure I got the softest, stinkiest, yummiest cheeses she had.

That morning, I approached the stall and patiently waited for pretty much every customer in town to leave. I did not want witnesses to the butchering I was about to do to their language. Finally, it was my turn.

I quietly launched into my prepared speech about wanting cheese, which was probably the most formal declaration of love she had ever heard in her life. I must have said the right thing, because before I knew it she had come around the counter and was force-feeding me small pieces of about 114 different kinds of cheese.

"*Si*," I'd say with a smile; or sometimes, with the most apologetic face I could muster, "*Non mi piace*." After she had wrapped up my selections and I paid her, I turned to leave and she waved and said, "*Ciao, bella*."

Now, this was a perfectly normal thing for her to say. She had probably said it 20 times that day. Everyone in Italy says it all the time, coming and going. I am sure she forgot about me four seconds after I left.

Miss Expatria

But even writing this now, three languages and five years later, it makes me teary. It was the first time an Italian had said it to me. Even though I was obviously not Italian, and had probably sounded like an injured seal, she said, "*Ciao, bella*" to me.

She was My First Italian, and I will never forget her.

Chapter Three

Before you judge me harshly as yet another American who hightailed it to Europe in search of bliss, I want to explain how I came to the point where I was buying cheese from a lady by the sea in Italy.

The problem is, I don't know where to begin.

Do I tell the story of my parents who, when I was six years old, moved from the suburbs of Philadelphia to their favorite vacation spot on the Jersey Shore? They taught me that it's in one's own power to find happiness, and there is no fear in changing the course of your life by doing something no one else around you has ever thought of doing.

Do I tell the story of working for a world-famous clothing designer? The first time I went to Europe was on his dime, and it opened the Pandora's box in me that is travel addiction. As his leather and suede expert - don't ask, but not nearly as glamorous or naughty as it sounds - and completely in over my head, I attended the Semaine de Cuir, or Leather Week, in Paris (also not as glamorous or naughty as it sounds).

I checked into the ridiculously chic hotel and, armed with my high school French and a corporate expense account, navigated the Paris Metro to the exhibition hall. After receiving my credentials I realized I was starving and quickly located the food stand, where I had my first meal in Europe: Brie and butter sandwich, glass of red wine. I laughed out loud at how utterly awesome Europe was.

When I returned to my hotel's neighborhood, which I now know was in the 1st arrondissement, I showered, changed and set out for my first evening in Paris. I walked around for over two hours, absolutely petrified to go into a restaurant and speak French to actual French people - to Parisians! I had just about given up hope of finding my courage and resigned myself to a night of room service and CNN when I saw the perfect bistro - quiet, friendly, and small.

My reaction to reading their menu was akin to what a 12-year-old boy must go through when he finds his older brother's porn stash. I called the waiter over - of course he was old, and had a bowtie and a long apron - and ordered every French food I had ever wanted to try. I'm sure he thought I was either expecting more people, or bulimic; but he dutifully filled the table with my dream food and with a "*bon appetit,*" left me to it.

Omelet, pate, mussels and fries, crème brulee - eating that meal was like seeing everything around me in Technicolor for the first time. I knew I had to get back to Europe as soon as possible and see what else I was missing.

But that was also the job that taught me perhaps my most important life lesson: It is in no way worth it to work 12-14 hours a day, 50 weeks a year, so that for only two weeks a year – and never, ever two consecutive weeks – you can live the life you want.

Do I tell the story of failing the Foreign Service exam by a tenth of a point? It made me realize that while I needed a way to support myself while I live abroad, I did not want to do so under increasingly dangerous conditions in countries I would never want to step foot in otherwise. My mom doesn't need to worry about me more than she already does.

I think the real story is that my entire life, for everything I ever set out to do, I get the desire, see the end result in my head, and somehow make it happen.

No, wait – "somehow" is a little too mysterious-sounding. I do a lot of research; I work out all the details; I keep it as my only focus for as long as it takes; and, I must admit, I am blessed with an incredible amount of luck.

§

I first visited Rome in late 1999, with Pavlov Memento and his sister. We rented an apartment near the Vatican for about a week, maybe longer. Our arrival was heralded by the airport losing his sister's luggage; her not understanding the concept of differences in time, currency or language; and Pavlov's attention deficit disorder in full swing. It was going to be a long vacation with these two.

On the morning of our first full day in Rome, Pavlov and his sister showered, dressed and went to the bar downstairs for coffee and waited for me to join them, which I did shortly after. I locked up the apartment with its one enormous, ancient key that looked as if it also fit the darkest dungeons of a medieval castle, skipped down the steps and opened the equally enormous, ancient door to the building.

And Rome hit me, full force; it was love at first sight, and it stopped me dead in my tracks.

Tiny, stooped old ladies in housecoats brushed past me with their shopping carts on their way to the outdoor market next to our building, and it was like a parade of my great-grandmother. Cars and mopeds screamed by, or were parked as if abandoned by bank robbers after a police chase. Spoons clattered onto ceramic plates and cups at the bar next door. Groups of men stood talking on the street, in the bar, at the market; I could not understand a word they were saying but they looked, acted and gestured exactly like my grandfather, every one of them, no matter their age.

But it wasn't just that everyone I saw looked like my family; it wasn't that it was oh-so-Italian, like a movie; I cannot think back to that day and point to any one thing that made me fall in love. All I knew was, I was home – and there was nothing on earth that was going to stop me from living there.

Living in Paris had always been a dream of mine, but a far-off one. Rome seemed somehow doable. If Paris was the rich old aunt you saw for tea every Sunday who told you to sit up straight, Rome was the aunt who had partied with the Stones and snuck you into R-rated movies. I knew which one I preferred.

As soon as we got back to New York, I started making plans. I worked at an ad agency that had offices worldwide, so that's where I began. The absolutely pitiful Human Resources Director had no idea how to go about contacting her counterparts in Italy, or even what it was I wanted to ask them.

There also was the question of what I did at the agency, which no one, including myself, knew how to explain. I won't bother you with the details; suffice it to say that it had nothing to do with marketing, advertising or print production, and everything to do with keeping track of a lot of information and an ability to use Microsoft Excel in ways never seen before or since.

The thing I had going for me was that while no one could describe what I did, they knew that without me they would be in a lot of trouble. I used this to my advantage as I took each element of my job and figured out how I could make it work without actually being in the office.

We eventually got a new HR Director, and I tried my pitch with her. She was appalled by her predecessor and intrigued by my idea in equal measure. Over the next several months I kept her in the loop about my progress, and she helped me create a really impressive PowerPoint presentation for my bosses.

I don't know how I got the idea to be a virtual employee. We designed, produced and mailed out over half a billion credit card offers every year for our client - yes, hi, that was us - and my group was in print production, which is a very hands-on, old-school industry. I think a lot of the old timers thought I was insane, but everyone kept their minds wide open; I could not have done what I did without their support. I was very lucky to be working with a pretty close-knit, easy-going team, and they went out of their way to help me in any way they could.

I was close with my bosses as well, including the CFO of the company. They almost wet themselves laughing at my serious, professional presentation, and at the end of it told me that of course I could go and try it out. I was thrilled.

We agreed to do a trial run – I was to go on "vacation" to Rome again in August 2001, work from there, and then do another presentation after getting feedback from my group. Pavlov Memento and I found a great apartment near the Colosseum online, booked it, and off we went.

We found an Internet place right near the apartment, on via S. Agata de Goti. They had just opened and were very amenable to my plugging in the laptop and sitting there for a few hours a day in silence. Pavlov used that time to run around the city, and would come flying back through the door several times while I was working to tell me what he had seen and done; but to be honest I was so focused on making my plan work, I can barely remember him being there.

We checked out of the apartment on September 11, and took a train to Anzio to spend a few quiet days of actual vacation on the beach before flying out on the 14th.

You know what happened next.

Miss Expatria

We wound up staying there until almost the end of September, when British Airways could fit us on a flight back through London. It was after the Italian holiday season so the hotel was empty except for the evenings, when out of nowhere busloads of Germans would show up for the dinner service, stay the night and leave around sunrise. But all day, every day, we had the run of the place – even if we could manage little more than watching CNN, staring into space, or walking to the beach and back.

The staff at that hotel was unbelievably kind. No matter how long it took to tear ourselves away from the TV in our room, they waited until we left to clean up. They brought us trays of food and drinks wherever we wound up sitting for more than 20 minutes at a time, since we were generally unfit for being in a public dining room with 150 Germans. And when I read them a teary thank you I had written in Italian, they hugged and kissed us and presented us with gifts from Anzio's anniversary celebration earlier that year.

I almost didn't go back to the States. I ate Valium like they were hard candy, and still managed a full-scale nervous breakdown at Heathrow during our layover.

When we did finally make it back I commenced my long, painful breakup with New York and prepared to flee to the welcoming arms of my new love, the one who cared for me when I thought all was lost: Rome.

Chapter Four

Fast-forward one year:

I've been teaching myself Italian for 80 minutes each day, during my daily commute between Westchester and Midtown Manhattan; I've read every single web page dedicated to expatriate life in general, and life in Italy in particular; I've packed up 58 boxes of belongings and placed them in storage, never knowing when I'd get to them again; I've visited the Italian consulates in two states and called the rest, and no one knows how I can legally live in Italy; I've researched the sizes of bed sheets and the wattage of light bulbs; I've negotiated a monthly rate with the tiny Internet point in Rome and had my company sign off on a final freelance agreement.

Pavlov Memento, meanwhile, partied like a man going to prison and staying away for days at a time. He insisted he could get by in Rome with his street Spanish. He had no idea where, or even if, he could work. He never wanted to talk about anything regarding the move. He was such a delight.

I asked him a million times: Are you sure you want to do this? And he always answered: Yes, I swear I am ready, this is going to be great. But his actions continued to speak more eloquently than he ever could, even on his best day.

Miss Expatria

Finally, it was the weekend before we were to leave for good. Our plan was to drive on Sunday to Cherry Hill, NJ, to my Aunt Dot's house - The Head Aunt, as I call her, as she is the matriarch of my father's side of the family - for one last goodbye with her, my parents, and a small gathering of relatives. We would bring the last of the storage boxes to give to my parents, then drive back to New York and check into a hotel for our remaining time there - and celebrate a final few days in the town we would never call home again.

Saturday night, no Pavlov. No phone calls, no text messages, nothing - until I received a drunken, slurred, incomprehensible voicemail from which I was able to surmise that he would be home in time to take me to Aunt Dot's.

A crucial factor in this story is that I don't drive; I have very poor depth perception, and I just plain suck at it. I took my test; the instructor gave me my license only after I promised that I would never get behind the wheel of a car ever, ever again - a promise I gladly have kept to this day.

The night came and went, as did most of the morning. Finally, another phone call - if I would lay out clothes for him he would come in, get ready, and we could go. He admitted he had not been to sleep, and would probably take a nap once we got to Aunt Dot's.

A nap. In the middle of a lunch being given in our honor. Classy.

Miss Expatria

He arrived home about 15 minutes before we had to head out again. He undressed and got in bed. He was tired, he said. He needed to sleep.

I was standing there, fully dressed, bag in hand, ready to go. Pavlov! Get up! We have to go now!

I'm tired. I just need to sleep.

Come on, this is the last thing we have to do, this is our last obligation and then we are home free. I need you to keep it together for, like, eight more hours. Come on, please, you can do this, we'll do it together.

He reached over and picked up his pants off the floor. He took out his wallet and threw money at my feet. Don't speak to me about obligations, he said. Take a taxi. I'm not going.

At that moment, as I stood at the edge of the bed, tears coming, crumpled-up money in my hand, the burden of my seven-year relationship with Pavlov Memento fell from the sky and landed on my shoulders with a weight I had never known was possible. For seven years, I had made excuses for his ignorance; I had defended him when others said he wasn't good enough; I showed him worlds he would have never known otherwise.

And he wanted to sleep.

I left the house, and you KNOW I slammed that door.

Miss Expatria

Outside on the stoop I called John, town taxi driver and personal friend of Jesus. I knew him well from all the times he had taken me up the hill for the train station late at night. He knew my voice right away.

"Cherry Hill? New *Jersey?!* Uhhhh…sure. I'll be there in five."

I held it together until he arrived; but as soon as I closed the door behind me and told him to head for the Turnpike, the stress of the entire last year came out in sobbing waves of anger, frustration and humiliation.

Let it out, John kept saying in his Jesus-loves-me joyous way. You can do better than that! Let me hear some real crying! Come on! I choked on my own laughter through the sobs.

Some time after we had crossed into New Jersey, I calmed down enough tell John what had happened. He already knew us, and of our plans to move to Rome ("God's living room," as he liked to call it). So I only had to start from the previous day.

John listened quietly as he navigated his way through tollbooths and past 18-wheelers. And when I finished, he asked if he could speak candidly.

"Of course," I said, and patiently waited for him to tell me that Jesus loves me.

"You know you can leave him, right? You aren't obligated to take him with you. It's your dream. It's your life."

Miss Expatria

§

When trying to show the visceral effect of driving their product, car commercials use a cinematic trick in which they make it seem like the street on which the car is driving suddenly flips over, revealing a long ribbon of empty road winding through majestic scenery.

It's a pretty cool special effect. But, imagine for a moment if that really happened to your world; close your eyes and try to see the scenario in your mind - after a grueling day at work, you're stuck in endless traffic during a rainstorm on your way to the supermarket at an hour when you know the lines are going to be out the door. It feels like time has stopped, leaving you forever trapped in the bleakest of moments.

Then, in front of your unbelieving eyes and faster than you can blink, everything you see in front of you flips over like a pancake; instead of being in congested rush-hour hell, you're driving down a quiet lane that leads to your favorite vacation spot.

And it's happened so quickly and effortlessly; it feels like the most logical thing in the world and very, very right. Every negative thing that only seconds before had been defining your life has been banished from your world. You realize where you are and know that after the next bend in the road, you're going to reach the place you dream of in your darkest hours.

That is exactly what happened to me.

Miss Expatria

The sputtering ticker tape of anxiety was silenced. My entire body relaxed. In that moment my entire world changed, and I felt myself become a finely tuned instrument of stunning beauty and unspeakable power.

I took out my phone, called Pavlov and, full of calm logic and devoid of any hysteria, ended it.

When I hung up, John took his eyes off the road long enough to find me in his rearview mirror. No words were exchanged; we nodded to each other, and he returned his gaze to the road.

Jesus totally loves me.

I arrived at Aunt Dot's to a flurry of hugs and noise. When the dust had settled, my father looked past me to the empty driveway.

"Where's Pavlov Memento?"

"I left him."

"Ha! No, really, where is he?"

"I left him."

For the first time in American history, a room full of South Philly Italians went silent. Everyone froze in place as my clear, calm, quiet voice repeated the unthinkable.

"Dad, I'm serious. I left him."

Miss Expatria

The room burst into life with questions, confusion, and the undeniable excitement that accompanies a juicy turn of events. Through the melee, I saw my mother standing apart from everyone, her hand frozen mid-dig in her purse, searching my face. We held that moment until I turned away to receive hugs from my Aunt Marion.

As the excitement evolved from talking to a flurry of chatty activity in the preparation of lunch, my mother motioned for me to follow her outside for a smoke.

She didn't take her eyes off me for the entire time it took her to walk to the edge of the driveway, find her cigarettes, take one out, light it, and take the first drag.

Normally, I'd be terrified of a moment like that. Everyone knows that when your mom takes you away from the relatives to a secluded spot and waits to speak until she's started on her cigarette, you're in for it. Rash decisions are non-existent in my family. But I knew I had done the right thing, and I would defend it to the death.

Finally, she spoke.

"You know I'm not the biggest fan of Pavlov." She took another drag.

I waited. Many, many conversations with my mother had started with this understatement.

"But I could see that you made each other happy, and when you cooked up this dream to move to Rome, I was happy you were not going to do it alone."

Another drag; she watched the smoke float away. I couldn't take my eyes off her.

"If you had called instead of coming here today, and told me over the phone that you'd left him, you probably would have given your father a second heart attack, and I would have been sick with worry."

Yet another understatement from the woman who called to make sure I was OK every time she saw an episode of *Cops*, which she calls, "Bad Boys Bad Boys."

"But I am standing here looking at you, and you're actually glowing. I haven't seen that for a long, long time. You actually look different! If you jumped up and flew over this house right now, it wouldn't surprise me in the least. I can see that you know you made the right decision. And I want you to know that because I've seen you today, and I can see your strength and your confidence, I am not going to worry one little bit while you're over there. I'm going to be pulling for you, and cheering you on. I cannot wait to hear all about your new, exciting life."

I think I actually grew taller. I, too, felt like I could take flight at any moment. I hugged her tight.

"Now, go back inside and let me finish my cigarette. I want to have a good mom cry, and if you're standing here I'll never stop."

Chapter Five

I took the regional train to and from Rome every day to go to work at the Internet point on via S. Agata de Goti. It was called Romalife, and you had to descend four steps to enter. The place was painted an angry, dark blue, lit with a 60-watt bulb, and there were six ancient computers set up on cold steel tables: two rows of two facing the door, and two more in their own private cubbies along the right side. I set up my laptop connection at a counter in front of the cubbies, closer to the door. I was the first person you saw coming in, as the register was on the left behind a steel bookshelf filled with dusty computer accessories for sale.

I came in about 1PM every day and worked until about 6:30 – I had to make sure I caught the train that met the last local shuttle of the night in Lavinio at 8PM. If I wanted to stay in town later than that, I'd either have to try my luck with the town taxi driver, who was always either eating or watching soccer and couldn't be bothered; walk home three kilometers; or spend the night in Rome.

Luckily, I had no friends and nowhere to be at night other than an occasional dinner with Hank and Chiara, so I had no problem getting that last train - until I received a dinner and sleepover invitation from the guy who ran the Internet point.

Miss Expatria

Marco was around my age and reminded me of an overgrown, mischievous altar boy. He greeted me warmly every day and over those first few months, became my first true friend in Rome. He spoke English pretty well and was patient with our language barrier; he knew when to correct me and when to let me keep talking because it was more important for me to get my message across than to say it 100 percent correctly.

Because Romalife was on a tiny side street and frankly looked uninviting, there were not many customers; Marco and I often found ourselves alone in there. If work was slow, I'd sometimes sign off early and we'd go grab a prosecco, a bite of pizza or a treat from some little place it seemed only Marco knew about.

More often than not, though, his two friends Giovanni and Vincenzo stopped by and hung out, downloaded music, and made each other cry with laughter. If anything makes you want to learn a foreign language, it's a room full of people cracking each other up.

Giovanni was tiny, cherubic; I came to find that his acerbic wit was a legally registered lethal weapon. He usually stopped at the top of the stairs upon his arrival and proclaimed something in his most serious voice, and they'd fall over laughing. I love people like this, and I wanted to be his friend more than anything.

Vincenzo had kind, dreamy eyes and spoke softly, but had a way of telling a story that absolutely debilitated Marco and Giovanni.

Miss Expatria

Giovanni could understand most of what I said in English if I spoke slowly and distinctly, but his tendency was to answer in German, which is the only other language he speaks; Vincenzo… well, here is a list I made in my journal one day:

Vincenzo's current English vocabulary:

Maybe baby shoes
Sexy
Happiness
I like you
Shit
Please get off
Danger
Love
Fashion
Erotical, eroginal zones
Birds
Boyfriend
Tank you Indians, tank you Terrence (sung to Thank U, by Alanis Morrisette; the actual words are, "Thank you India/Thank you terror")
Brunch
Beautiful

Needless to say, we stuck to Italian.

As we got to know each other better, they were horrified when I told them of my solitary nights in silent, empty Lavinio. Marco hatched a plan for me to come in to Rome on Saturday night, go out to dinner with him and Vincenzo and then crash at Vincenzo's, where Marco also was living at the time.

The thought of actually spending an entire evening with only Italians and speaking only Italian was terrifying and thrilling; I hadn't been out in so long, and I was so touched by their invitation. I hesitated and stammered a bit as I accepted.

They misread my reaction as my accepting a date with Marco. And that is when, in one fell swoop, a room full of gay men came out to me.

I already knew they were gay, so I had no idea why they were telling me right then, and I got all flustered and confused. I'm sure you can guess the hilarity that ensued as we cleared up the miscommunication.

We had a great time that weekend, although it was exhausting to concentrate so hard on the language - listening comprehension is my worst language skill. I got home on Sunday afternoon and slept until Monday morning; I arrived at Romalife on Monday afternoon to find that I had become the unofficial doyenne of my very own gay mafia.

§

I don't know if I did anything in particular to warrant my role as the gay mafia's pet project. But they were hell-bent on getting me into Rome; I had to move out of my place after the New Year holiday anyway - and so it began.

Miss Expatria

Every Tuesday and Friday I would walk to the newsstand in Piazza Madonna di Monti and buy *Porta Portese*, the classified ads paper for Rome that shares its name with the world-famous weekly flea market. I would come into Romalife, spread out a map of Rome, and start reading the classifieds. Marco helped me with the abbreviations and wording; I'd call out names of neighborhoods and they would yea-or-nay each one, and depending on that we'd read futher about the particulars of the apartment for rent.

Most Roman neighborhoods are named after their main church, so sometimes I'd be calling out 10 or 15 saints' names in a row. Vincenzo found this hilarious; thus, my search for apartments usually went like this:

"San Lorenzo?"

"Prega per noi." ("Pray for us.")

"Santa Maria Maggiore?"

"Prega per noi."

"San Giovanni?"

"Prega per noi."

… until Marco would laughingly tell him to shut up and help me.

I finally found a tiny studio apartment on via Belisario, just south of the museum side of Villa Borghese park. I went to see it alone and met My Second Italian: Alessio, Hot Landlord.

When I went to sign the six-month lease, I brought Vincenzo with me to make sure everything was on the up-and-up – and to have him tell me if Alessio was gay or not. I couldn't tell and just had to know, for my own sake.

We went to his apartment – or, as is the Italian way, his family's apartment that he still lived in with his entire family. It was beautifully decorated and the largest apartment I had ever seen in a major city. We sat around the formal dining room table with Alessio and his mother, and she patiently read the simple lease and explained what everything meant. Vincenzo was enamored of her elegance and insured me that it was OK to sign it. He also gave me the high-sign that Alessio was indeed playing for my team.

After everything was official, Alessio's mom busted out the family's homemade limoncello, and we all toasted to my first real apartment in Rome.

§

2005-03-03 Notes from Lavinio, Dec. 2002

This is a list I wrote to inspire me, and to stop the downward spiral into madness from the scirocco.

The scirocco is a months-long, non-stop, wet, howling wind that comes from Africa, dumping a ton of sand everywhere and making it impossible to dry your clothes, especially if you live on the sea like I did at the time. I was perpetually

Miss Expatria

touching, smelling, turning, futzing with my soggy laundry and sweeping the floors to be rid of the sand.

And trying, desperately, to tune out the howling of that maddening wind.

In my new life:

I wear perfume every day
I know Rome inside and out
I drink red wine every day
I express myself in Italian
I go to Paris for the weekend
I am Coco Chanel, Babe Paley and Katherine Graham
I influence opinion
I cook well
I walk around Venice and do not speak to anyone
I spend time in the place where my great grandfather was born
I keep a record of my new life
I take pictures
I hear stories from old people
I see the sun set over the horizon, not over buildings
I remember God more
I keep laughing
I use Christmas lights and candles to light a room
I travel to India and Africa

With the exception of traveling to India and Africa, I've done pretty well with this list.

§

Miss Expatria

The gay mafia came to collect me and my things from Lavinio; Hank was there to bid me farewell and to make sure we didn't steal anything. I'm not sure he knew what to make of the guys.

All of us crammed into Vincenzo's tiny Fiat Punto, laughing, chatting, smoking, answering cell phones, Marco yelling when Vincenzo made a wrong turn that took us toward Napoli.

My life was beginning.

Chapter Six

I think my first six months in Rome can be summed up best in my own words at the time.

2003-03-01

I went to pick up my pants today; I just love the couple that runs the tiny, battered, cluttered tailor shop. When I arrived the husband was outside checking a thread in the sunlight, squinting and turning.

I went in and we all chatted for a while; a lot of storeowners do this once they've seen you a couple times. It's like you dropped by to see them, and you just happen to need something that they provide. They were watching one of those horrible variety shows that entertain Italian people in some indefinable way. This particular show is like if Tom Jones and Carmen Electra had a show, and they sang *Home on the Range*.

They seem highly amused that I am American and when I dropped the pants off last week, the wife and I had a long discussion about THE WAR. Everyone here, upon finding out I am American, asks me who I like better - CLEEENTONE OR BOOOSH. They all love Clinton, and are so thrilled to hear that I love him, and then they proceed to spout off about THE WAR. One woman confided in me that she didn't trust Bush: His eyes were too close together.

Anyway, they loved that I didn't know the song they were singing on this show. I sang part of an old Italian song I learned growing up, and it was all in dialect; they fell over laughing, but I think they were impressed as well.

It was one of those Rome days, where everything I saw and everyone I interacted with was wrapped in light and quintessential and airy and like the opening scene to a movie.

2003-03-04

It is gorgeous today, not a cloud in the sky and probably 65. Everyone is still wearing their huge puffy coats because *God forbid* they feel a chill; but at least they have done away with scarves, gloves, and hats.

I just came back from standing outside with Marco, Luca and Eleonora, smoking and cracking each other up, and it occurred to me that I am so thankful for moments like that, of standing around with other people, no longer the outsider, we're all just friends hanging together.

2003-03-05

Today the gay mafia was all atwitter about this year's *San Remo* show, and before I knew it Vincenzo and I were dashing off to get provisions for a dinner with Marco, Giovanni, and another member of the gay mafia, Remo. We went to Todis supermarket - three bottles of wine, two bottles of water, eggs, pasta, sausage, potatoes, and cheese for 20 euro. I just laughed and handed over my card.

Miss Expatria

The checkout ladies in the supermarkets here are an interesting bunch. They're generally in their 50s, and under their smocks they are dressed to the nines, and they talk nonstop - to each other across the aisles, to the customers, about the customers, about anything and everything. And they never miss a beat, which is good because it gets you in and out quickly; but it forces you to pay attention to everything they say in case they are talking to you.

"So I told Antonio to pick up the chairs from Simone and he tells me do you have a discount card? You! Discount card? No? He says he has to go get his mother at four, so there is no way he can how many bags do you need? He can't be there in time, so I had to call Antonella, you know, the one who lives 14 euro 62 please. Thank you she lives up the block do you have 18 cents?"

I have discovered why storeowners and cashiers are constantly asking for complicated combinations of change - apparently, the banks are a mess so no one ever goes to get their daily till. Paradoxically, the cash machines here usually spit out only 50 euro notes. I can't count the number of times I've gotten things for free, or have had to buy more than what I needed, simply because the store didn't have change.

Anyway, back to *San Remo*.

Vincenzo and I started cooking (and eating and drinking) before Marco closed up Romalife and arrived with

Miss Expatria

Giovanni and Remo in tow. We wound up wearing aprons, turbans and sunglasses by the time they all got there.

Vincenzo hung up some leftover Christmas lights, lit a bunch of candles and set the table beautifully, with dried peperoncino and walnuts and apples; all the plates and silverware matched (which is a feat for his motley collection of kitchenware).

I love him. He is heavy into making everything just right, and he has that kind of small-town Southern Italian old lady-ness that makes everything so... quaint is too condescending a word. You know what I mean? When you go into an old lady's home in Italy and she has strange things displayed that you would never have in your house, but the cumulative affect of it makes you want to die from the cuteness?

Then the show started. OH MY GOD.

All the songs are original, and the contestants are split into two categories - already famous singers, and young unknown singers. It was four hours long and tacky as hell, and followed up with a dopofestiva, in which all the singers, journalists, and various hangers-on had a kind of warped academic discussion about the show. The singers sat at tables toward the back of the stage, and in the middle of the show, waiters brought out food and wine for everyone, and they were taking phone calls that were answered like they were in their home ("Hello. Who is this? Hold on a second.").

Miss Expatria

Apparently this goes on every night until Friday, with the dopofestiva and everything, and then Saturday the winners from the previous nights sing their songs again for some sort of prize.

The entire evening ended at 2AM, when Vincenzo drove me home. I didn't even pull out the bed; I slept right on the couch, like the dead, until I awoke like a princess at noon today. Then when I got to work there was a package from Jackie! FDNY calendars for the boys and a New York Times (2/28) for me!

Jackie - Jax, I call her - is yet another friend I made from my job. She is the receptionist, and I barely knew her as she was stationed on a different floor and so we didn't receive packages or guest calls from her. When I was preparing for my move, several people told me that Jackie had been to Rome, and that she, too wanted to move there.

News of my impending move brought out the dreamer in everyone. They'd sigh, get a far-off look and say, "I'd love to live in Rome, too." So, I didn't make an extra effort to talk to Jackie about it.

Then one night after work a big gang went out to celebrate something - a birthday or, more likely, someone having quit - and Jax and I found ourselves at a small table together. Purely to make conversation, I told her that I had heard about her interest in Rome.

"Oh yeah! I spent a year in Padova, and then tried to find a job in Rome - but I never did, and then 9/11 happened, and I came back home."

"You've actually lived in Italy? Wait, you were there for 9/11? So was I!"

"No way! Hey, did you hear that song all the time... how does it go... *Dammi tre parole...*"

"*...Sole cuore amore...*"

And then both of us together, like long lost twins that had been reunited at last, "*Dammi un bacio che non fa parlare!!!*"

And a friendship was born.

I can't wait til she comes over to visit - it'll be a relief since she speaks Italian about a million times better than I do. She'll get along famously with the guys, and she'll be able to translate all the stupid things I want to say but haven't yet found the words.

2003-03-06

Another beautiful day here: cloudless, warm, perfect.

Usually I leave my house to go to work when everyone else is leaving work to go to lunch, unless I am up early and running errands. Today there were so many sights, sounds, smells that took me to other places and times; it threatened to overwhelm me with thoughts of my old life, far away.

All the restaurants and bars have their doors and windows open, and I could hear the clinking of silverware and plates and restaurant noise. Like the first time Pavlov Memento and I went to Paris: We got off one stop too far and had to walk the long way down Avenue Bosquet to our hotel. He was in awe of everything he saw; I wanted to cry, because he got it, his heart was hurting from the beauty just like mine did when I first went there. Anyway, we got there at lunchtime, and those sounds were everywhere on that street.

The feel and smell of the weather brings me home to the Jersey Shore, to the owners coming down to open up their houses on the first nice weekend; the first time you can wear shorts, and they're all wrinkled and ill-fitting and your legs are green they are so pale; the ocean still being FREEZING; Mack and Manco's pizza shop taking out their storm windows; and even further back in my mind to prom dates and gym classes held outside.

Around the corner from Romalife on via Baccina there was the smell of baking bread, which took me back to living in TriBeCa; walking from the loft through Chinatown, Little Italy and the Lower East Side to my old job at the school, and all the discoveries I made about New York 10 years after moving there.

And then I arrive at work, and I am shoved back into the present: Here are Marco and Vincenzo, laughing, going through our repertoire of private jokes. And I am filled with so much love for them and for myself and for my life that it is overwhelming me, I have to put my Jackie O sunglasses back on.

2003-03-12

The gay mafia has never heard of *In Your Eyes* by Peter Gabriel, let alone heard it; his most famous song here is *Shock the* FRICKING *MONKEY*. WHAT??

2003-03-13

Marco just correctly conjugated a verb for me that I have totally gotten wrong since Day One. I feel like a dumbass and no doubt have sounded like one as well, as I use this verb all the time.

Oh well. Another lesson; put it on my tab.

2003-03-14

Today was another transit strike, both buses and metro. I knew it the second I got to the stop near my house - there weren't any buses all the way up the street, and it was quieter. I called Marco and he confirmed: SCIOPERO!

I love the strikes, even though they are dreadfully inconvenient. I love that they have a starting time and ending time, so you can plan your day around them. The newspaper actually prints the Italian strike schedule ahead of time. I think this one today lasts until 4:30, so I should be OK for the ride home.

Miss Expatria

2003-03-15

I made a huge American breakfast for Marco and Remo today!

While I had my morning cig I worked on translating the instructions for the pancake mix I bought. I wanted to make sure they didn't say anything weird or too different. Only after I had read it through and looked up some words, did I see it in English on the side of the box.

We had pancakes, eggs, French toast, bacon, and OJ. They loved it, and demanded more French toast. It was so weird to have those tastes and smells here. I was serving it as each piece was done (two frying pans), and they had no idea how to eat it - they were picking up the French toast with their fingers, and rolling the pancakes up like crepes after stuffing them with bacon.

Then I made Remo his first PB&J sandwich, and he was falling all over the couch, "Buono, buonissimo!" I can't imagine never having had a PB&J sammie before. He thought it was a normal dessert one had after brunch; I told him it was what many children have for lunch every day as a main course. They were aghast.

2003-03-19

I love going to see the Pope at the Vatican. I like that it is an atmosphere without either subversion or fanaticism. Just people, happy to be Catholic, and there to see their guy. In the summer the Pope flies overhead in his helicopter from Castel Gandolfo, like a rock star, and people are cheering and the Mexicans are always singing and chanting. He rides around in the Popemobile right up onto the stage, and everyone goes crazy.

Then the cardinals get up and speak in their native language, telling the Pope about whatever guests are there, like, the PTA from St. Whosmawhatsis in Wherevertown, and you hear a tiny cheer or song come through from this immense crowd.

It really is quite moving.

2003-03-20

I should have known what today was going to be like when my laundry lady kept me for a half hour, screaming about BOOOSH.

I was waiting for my bus with some people, who eventually became more people, but no buses arrived. Finally, just as we saw an ENORMOUS crowd turn the corner up at the other end of via XX Settembre, a guy came by and said there were protests ("manifestazioni") everywhere. The group we were now seeing approach was going to the British Embassy at Porta Pia, at our end of the street. Everyone threw their hands up in the air and started calling and texting; I walked to work.

When I got there the connection was down, so Giovanni bought some spumante from the bar in the piazza and we drank "for peace." I finally had to go over to another Internet place on via Cavour to work there, and I sat facing the huge window on via Cavour.

Miss Expatria

Over the top of my screen I see the Carabinieri come up the street, turning back traffic. I go outside to see what's up and there are 10,000 people at the end of via Cavour, waiting to march. At the same moment, Marco texted me to say the connection was back up at his place. I pulled the plugs, not bothering to shut down, and beat it across via Cavour just as they were approaching.

2003-03-22

Last night we went to this tiny, dingy, green-tiled place with great food. Vincenzo had to keep getting up and going over to the table where the owner and his cigar presided to give our orders, and they had lengthy conferences about each dish. Everyone in the place ordered that way. No one seemed to mind.

Then we went to the late night bakery and had piping hot, fresh pastry smothered in white chocolate. We stayed there a while and rated the guys behind the counter and caused minor disturbances. Then we went driving around in Vincenzo's car, and he berated me for not having seen more of Rome.

I came home happy, full, buzzed, tired, loved.

Saw Alessio, Hot Landlord this morning to give him the rent. He came to the apartment and was very curious about my pictures of Katherine Graham, Babe Paley and Coco Chanel. Please God forgive me for likening William Paley to Silvio Berlusconi; I don't know the Italian word for media king. I am sure he was thoroughly confused.

Miss Expatria

2003-03-28

While walking to work today I overshot the hill crossing, so I had to walk through the dreaded tunnel that runs underneath Quirinale, where the President lives. With my horrible lack of depth perception, it felt like a million hot, smelly miles.

I find it strange that a working tunnel can go under a president's house; it seems kind of unsafe to me.

When I got to work, Marco was leaving to return Alfio's car to Luca and Alfio. Luca and Alfio are a couple, and in the gay mafia, to be sure; but they're so awesome and cool, I always feel like I have to be on my best behavior when I'm around them for some reason. Of course, this makes my Italian worse and I always wind up messing up what I'm saying. This appears to amuse them, so I guess it's OK; but it makes me want to say to them, *NO, wait, really I'm cool, I swear, if only you knew me in English!*

I decided to join Marco and as we were ready to leave Giovanni walked up, so he came along, too. We drove around for what seemed like an hour (we had to keep doubling back to find the right entrance); finally we made it to Luca and Alfio's new apartment, in a newly renovated former industrial bakery. It's like L.A. meets Miami meets the Love Boat - arches and nautical-style railings and everything is crisp and white and new. They have a cool apartment, very loft-like, overlooking the trains into Termini. And they have an awesome roof terrace, all sky;

you can see the Castelli Romani - the hills that surround Rome to the south - and the tiny villages perched up there.

Amidst dust, workmen and detritus we sat down to a lovely lunch. Everything just happened; so casual, so spur of the moment, so effortless, so them. Then this other guy came in. I do not know who he was, but he sat near the table on a stepladder, smoked incessantly, said little, and then did the dishes.

It was another enchanted day with my friends.

2003-03-29

Brunch went smashingly today at Luca and Alfio's new place: Light streaming in, talking, laughing, everyone smoking cigarettes, trains going by, Luca cutting everyone's hair, them making fun of me for doing the dishes like a housewife, the difference between portabile/portatile, more talking, more laughing, Alfio messing up the coffee and starting over, everything so easy breezy.

They had heard about *broonch* from Marco and Remo and again, no one had any idea how to eat it; but eat it they did, in their own way - taco-style, with everything piled into a pancake, rolled up and shoved right on in. In addition, Marco made everyone brie, bacon, cream cheese (simply called "Philadelphia" here, like Band-Aids and Q-Tips for us) and maple syrup sandwiches. They thought these were delightful as well. I laughed, thinking of what New Yorkers would make of such a calorie bomb.

Miss Expatria

2003-04-01

Signore H. is pronounced Signore "Acca," as H is said in Italian. I have no idea what he does, but Signore H. has some sort of studio on the same street as Romalife; he knows everyone and everything, and he has this awesome old dog named Pallina that follows him everywhere, who also knows everyone and everything.

Last night Signore H., like many older people in the neighborhood do, had Marco type up a hand-written letter for him and print out two copies. Pallina came in, looked around a little, sniffed her apparent disapproval, and then went out and laid on the stoop. I love this dog.

Zoe is another dog that lives on the block. She is a Boxer puppy - although she's nearly as big as Pallina - and thinks everything is just dandy. Her poor owners - a beautiful family who live across the street from Romalife - are constantly being dragged hither and yon as Zoe finds yet another fascinating hubcap, food wrapper or puddle that is the best hubcap, food wrapper or puddle she has ever seen. She gets equally excited when we call her name - *they know me!* - and comes bounding over to say hi.

2003-04-02

Helicopters are directly over my apartment building, in their flight pattern between the British and U.S. embassies. Their blade shadows are cutting through the sunlight that this time of year comes onto my windowsill and my new plants.

The noise is enough to make me insane. It is loud, persistent, ominous. I can hear the speeches through the bullhorns, and the cheers. Please, make it stop.

Here's the government:

"We will bomb the shit out of Iraq while you stand around and sing 'Imagine' off-key and wear old army jackets."

Here's the protesters:

"IMAGINE AALLLL THE PEEEEEEEPUUUUULLLL."

I guess everyone has their uniform, right? The protesters and the military. I wonder what would happen if a deafening crowd of well-dressed business people started protesting the war?

2003-04-07

Since Sunday morning I have been breaking the First Commandment and worshipping at the altar of MY NEW PURSE. It is a stunning, breathtaking vintage Kelly bag (not Hermes, but even BETTER) of the most luminous and creamy brown leather. AND I GOT IT FOR 20 EURO at Porta Portese.

First off, I was looking at books, as part of my new learning regimen, and the book vendor had this antique hatbox for 5 euro that I bought. LIKE I NEED A HAT BOX. But this one is not flimsy; it is made of forest green canvas and trimmed in brown leather with a brown leather belt buckle-type closure. And the inside is green silk. Oh, and I bought a book written in Italian about American culture.

OK, so I am still walking around and BAM THERE IS THE BAG STARING AT ME LONGINGLY, so what else could I do but return the stare. Luckily I had on my Jackie O sunglasses so the old man couldn't see my eyes literally fill up with tears (at this point I had 10.42 euro on me).

I asked to see it and his nasty wife pulled it off the wall and flung it at me. The man said it was 20 euro and I almost threw up, because if I had had the cash on me I would have bought it without haggling. I said it was beautiful and gave it back. When I shook my head in utter despair, he went down to 15.

Now I really am ready to throw up. He was insisting and I told him it was beautiful but I only had 10.42 euro on me. This made the wife apoplectic but the man says, you can have the bag and come back with the rest of the money.

I almost died. I think I actually swooned. The wife seemed to be ready to file for divorce. I gave him all the money I had and told them I would be back next Sunday with the 5 euro. The wife flat out did not believe me and said so, but the old man knew I'd come back.

I went all the way home that instant, got my back card, took money out, and went back to the place within two hours and gave him not five but 10 euro. The wife managed to stay pissed off anyway, I guess for proving her wrong. The man was clearly gloating and seemed to know I was going to pay the original price. I count him among my Roman Allies. I think he might have to be My Third Italian.

I think I might literally construct an altar to this bag. It is divine. It is like a holy relic from a more glamorous era. I think I could actually channel Grace Kelly through this bag.

In my frenzy, I did manage to notice at the market: Gorgeous antique furniture (note to self: Hit lottery, buy palazzo, furnish it from Porta Portese); a bakery that smelled like how heaven should smell; African peddlers being roughed up by cops; a beautiful four-star hotel on a sketchy dead-end street.

I walked slowly back across the river, and then strolled around - Pantheon, Piazza Navona, walked home. Found a place with the best torta della nonna EVER, fresh on a Sunday! Thought about my purse waiting for me at home; swooned.

2003-04-08

I was in Conad the other day and they sell Kraft Lunchables. This, apparently, is our big food contribution to Italy. Mortifying.

I love Conad, though; its official name, to me, is CONAD THE BEST STORE EVER. They have a little bit of everything - a big draw in a city where, in some neighborhoods (i.e., mine), you still have to go to the cheese store, the butcher, the bakery, etc. for your groceries. Also, because they are in Termini they're open throughout the day - no lunch break - and later at night than normal stores.

I do love how the daily rhythm of my life has changed in order to accomodate shop owners who still see lunch with the family and a little pisolino (nap) as a higher priority than staying open for the lunchtime customer. And, who doesn't love opening a dozen little paper-wrapped presents - sometimes with ribbon! - upon returning home with the day's purchases?

But the American in me takes much pleasure in being able to buy food, toiletries and alcohol all in one place, at good prices, at a time that's convenient for me. It's a huge treat for me, actually; I feel like I'm cheating the system somehow. Of all the things I'd guessed I'd miss from home, I never thought the discovery of a glorified bodega would send me into ecstasy.

2003-04-10

I went to Luca and Alfio's today to get my haircut. Luca was laughing but horrified at my tendency to take kitchen scissors to my hair when I have nothing better to do, or when I feel that a certain curl is not behaving. He suggested smoking a cigarette or going for a walk until the urge passes.

He fixed my hair as best he could and then blow-dried it straight. Marco and Vincenzo insist I look glamorous, but I think I look like a 55 year-old Republican. I am just happy not to look like Monica Lewinksy, whom I vaguely remember resembling the last time someone blow-dried my hair straight.

Luca and Alfio made pasta with pesto for lunch, and it was delicious as usual. Luca's dad in Verona made the pesto.

Luca told me that every time he thinks of us saying, ARE YOU POOPING IN YOUR PANTS the other night, he cracks up. I teach them horrible, horrible things to say in English. I can't help it; Luca somehow can do a perfect American accent but he can't understand much of what he's saying, and he's so handsome and suave - no one in America who looks like him would be caught dead saying, ARE YOU POOPING IN YOUR PANTS. I make him repeat things simply for my own amusement.

Oh, which reminds me - last night Marco and I went to the Ethioian place I love for dinner; so spicy and messy and delicious. The first time I ate African food of any kind was here, with the gay mafia. I thoroughly enjoy tasting things so different from my normal daily diet, here - things that don't have a base of garlic and olive oil and tomatoes. I'd love to hit a few places in New York, the next time I go back; but the menu is in Italian, so I don't know if I'd have any idea what anything was on an English Menu. Spriss Rosso? I don't think so.

Anyway, I forget what he was talking about but he meant to say "lawyers" and instead he said, in English, "lawns." I corrected him and he looked thoughtful for a moment, then asked, "What does it mean, 'The Hissing of Summer Lawns?'"

"Like the Joni Mitchell album?"

"Yes."

I explained in Engtalian what it meant - holy crap, was that hard, but he got it eventually and just continued to look at me. Then he asked me to repeat the word "lawyers." Then I had to spell them both. I finally asked him what was up.

He loves that Joni Mitchell album, and he wanted to know what the title meant. He looked up "lawns" in his translation dictionary, but it wasn't in there. He figured it was close enough to "lawyers," which was the next entry in the dictionary, to have to be some kind of derivative of "lawyers." So, this whole time, he has been thinking the title had to do with the HISSING OF SUMMER LAWYERS.

He also calls marshmallows, "Flushing Meadows" and puppies, "poopies." Far be it from me to correct him.

2003-04-11

Marco had to go somewhere this afternoon and left Vincenzo in charge of the shop; of course, 15 things happened. Vincenzo was in full panic mode, which for anyone else would be a step above comatose. He was kind of laughing and throwing his hands up and then coming over and hugging me, and asking me to talk to American tourists, and flitting around. He is much more masculine than I am making him out to be; but I wish I could remember him forever, just like he is today.

Miss Expatria

2003-05-05

Sunday, Part 1: Porta Portese.

I went looking for a gift for my dad's birthday, and alighted upon a table heaped with old letters, envelopes and postcards. It was just me and three philatelic freaks sifting through this mountain of mail. I finally found a hospital bill for a maternity stay, from the same week my father was born! She stayed for 11 days and paid, like, 10 bucks.

They sell every possible object at Porta Portese, with the exception of small electric fans. I CANNOT FIND SMALL ELECTRIC FANS, OR ANY FANS AT ALL, ANYWHERE IN THE CITY OF ROME.

I did, however, see a man selling puppies from a basket and I was extremely, dangerously close to buying one.

Sunday, Part 2: BEACH.

It's 6 euro and I got escorted to my very own lounge chair. My ticket said the price also included emergency services, lifeguards (apparently just for guarding your life, not for posing near your chair), and use of the lovely cabanas. It was about 10 degrees cooler than the city, sumptuous breezes, altogether perfect. I was there from 3-6 and got some luscious color on my skin. I cannot wait to go again, and again.

Miss Expatria

Beach, in comparison to Ocean City, where I grew up:

- Everyone comes to the beach fully dressed in street clothes, and then strips down or gets changed right there on the beach. In OC, we call these people "shoobies," or amateur beachgoers.

- No one is on a blanket on the sand; everyone uses the lounge chairs, which have their own little sunshades that come up over the back.

- I did not see many itsy bitsy suits on men, thank God, but also they have not gone the other way with those hellatiously long swim trunks guys wear in the U.S. now. Many people coming out of the shower cabanas in their FULL LENGTH TERRY CLOTH ROBES, acting like it's not sunny and 75.

- Some topless sunning, mostly by older women. Many, many fabulous accessories on the women, fully bejeweled, with layers of sarongs and wrapthings and lovely little chiffon numbers.

- Kids do not play in the sand, dig holes or do any general cavorting. There is a non-beachy play area, and they were basically all there.

- EVERYONE was chatting incessantly, which actually was really charming.

Sunday, Part 3: Chinese food with the gang, plus Claudio, a new addition.

Alessandro promised me that next time, we'll do Indian. He is such a total high maintenance Chelsea boy that it surprises me when he speaks in Italian. Unlike my core gay mafia guys, he's always dressed to the nines and has seen the inside of a gym recently. My guys aren't sloppy or overweight in the least; but they look like guy's guys, the kind of guys you'd have a beer with. Alessandro looks like, *get me a Cosmo, darling, and step on it.*

We were outside having a cig (we were at a non-smoking place for Lorenzo, Alessandro's boyfriend, who has asthma and also is allergic to pineapples), and who drives up but Vincenzo and his tiny, adorable, salty mother?

Vincenzo was taking his mom to the late night cornetto shop. This was about 12:30AM. She doesn't look AT ALL like the kind of woman you'd be taking to a late night bakery usually frequented by young people in various states of inebriation; but there she was, purse on her lap, smiling. The woman is always up for anything.

2003-05-08

I bought a fan yesterday! I got home last night, opened the box, and:

1. There were two fans in it.
2. Each fan was in 30 pieces.
3. The directions were in Korean.
4. There were no pictures or diagrams of any kind.

Miss Expatria

I extracted the pieces I needed, and last night MIT awarded me an honorary degree in Engineering after I put it together.

This morning I schlepped the other one back to the hardware store and luckily the two assholes from yesterday were not there (the one who flat-out ignored me, and the one who was quietly furious that I was interrupting his highly personal phone call); it was the nice cool guy who bagged it for me and a funny, round man. We just stood there and laughed about it in their tiny tiny place. The nice cool guy has promised to take me to breakfast at the bar next door whenever I want for being so honest.

This morning I took a long walk from the far end of Cola di Rienzo to Romalife. Observations:

- A woman in a motorino helmet fighting on the street with her grown son; he was furious and she was cool as a cucumber and so stylish; she got on her motorino and left him standing there in a fury, fabulous
- Gelato, half Nutella and half Gianduia
- Got a letter from my uncle, who is a retired bishop; he is very very old and his letter was a delightful, rambling history of Catholicism, his time in Italy and Rome in particular, and papal gossip
- So many fragrant trees
- Cola di Rienzo is blissfully free of tourists; Germans everywhere else
- A tour group, the leader of which used a rubber chicken speared onto a stick as her guide pole

- The little old lady who took the seat i offered her smiled; you could see what she looked like at 20
- A lot of stores playing Giorgia songs, she is like my soundtrack for living here. She has great pronunciation and a beautiful voice, so I sing along with her songs to help me pronunciate better. There's this one song she has, called Marzo (March, like the month), which has a refrain of, "Amami" ("Love me"). The "mi" part is carried out in ever-higher scales - *Amamiiiiiiiii* - and it annoys the guys so much whenever it comes on at Romalife. They've since substituted "Amami" with *sparami, scopami, salami,* and a variety of untranslatable rhymes.

2003-05-11

Marco and I went to Eleonora's sister's wedding at Campodoglio, Rome's city hall, at 9AM. It was in this official-looking room right off the piazza, all dark red silk damask walls and gold gilt chairs; it was like a courtroom placed inside a jewel box. Manuela was the first one to get married today; we saw two other brides and grooms go in and out after her as we milled around watching them get their photos taken.

Manuela's husband is very handsome. She is marrying him for love, but also so he can get his citizenship - he is Albanian.

Manuela's best friend also is named Manuela, and needs to have her own reality TV show. If she was American she might be in the trailer-trash category; she was definitely showing too much skin for a wedding (and for it being 9AM), and is a human firecracker.

Another woman showed up in a cherry red slinky dress, which made me inquire as to her relation to the bride and/or groom; Eleonora just rolled her eyes. Must get more on that. But apparently red is not the forbidden color at weddings here like it is in the U.S.

The whole wedding took about eight minutes and seemed to be a reading of constitutional articles regarding marriage. Oh, and? The official guy presiding over the wedding had on a huge green-red-white sash, like Roberto Benini did in *Life is Beautiful*.

To the left of that man behind her own dais was a haggard-looking yet strangely elegant woman who had a fan directed at her. She seemed to be in charge of stamping documents and also of the music, which apparently is used for every ceremony. It was some sappy love song on a cassette tape.

The entire thing was utterly surreal; I expected Fellini to come out and yell, CUT at any moment. (I just asked Vincenzo what a director says in Italian when the scene is done: STOP! Hahahahaha. But of course, it's pronounced STOPE. Oh, wait, now they're telling me it's TAGLIA, which literally means, "cut." I think I might have confused them.)

At the end of the ceremony, a man appeared from the back with some flowers for Manuela, and I whispered to Marco that they must be the official state flowers. We started laughing in the way that you laugh only in church or some other place where laughing really isn't appropriate. I do not think we ever recovered.

After we gave our congratulations and bid our goodbyes, we walked down the long path that overlooks the Forum and went to our favorite pasticceria; then we sat in our piazza for a while. We talked about Eleonora, who works at Romalife sometimes. She gives computer and Internet lessons in-house to people. She's so sweet, and quiet, and gentle; how she and Manuela grew up in the same house, I'll never know.

We were quiet for a while and then Marco said, "Here is my plan for the future" and I said, "One: Win the lottery." He goes, "Oh, I did already," and then told me the story about how he and Vincenzo won about $50,000 in the lottery in 1999. It was fascinating!

2003-05-12

Went to Ikea today and purchased a scale, an American-sized drinking glass and some other little odds and ends. Had an enormous fight with the shuttle bus driver, who said, "Ten minutes" when he pulled up to Ikea and came out a full 45 minutes later, picking his teeth, to find me and two old ladies with our bags, sweltering and fuming in the noon heat.

The fight was made all the more juicy by the fact that I had all that time to stand there and think of spectacular insults in Italian. We spent the five-minute ride back to the subway bickering, and then he asked me out on a date. I laughed and got off the bus with a wave over my shoulder.

"Ten minutes" - "dieci minuti" - I have discovered is a phrase used when one wants to say, "A little bit of time." Dieci minuti NEVER means ten actual minutes.

Ran home and threw on my bathing suit, then jumped on the ghetto train for a blissful late-afternoon collapse on the beach, from around 3 - 6:30.

Ran home again, jumped in the shower, and ran over to see Paul McCartney give his free concert outside the Colosseum. The whole street was packed from the Colosseum up to the Vittorio Emmanuele monument, and they had big TVs set up; via Cavour looked like Little Italy during the San Gennaro festival, with the... grease trucks I call them; they sell delicious, greasy grilled sausage or pork sandwiches.

The best part of the whole concert: His first three songs were what I came to hear - two Beatles songs and that one, I do not know why I like it, maybe because the words (as I hear them) are so bizarre – *I thought the maaajor was a laaady suff-re-gette*?

Home and blissfully in bed by 11, reading John Grisham in Italian and drifting off into sleep.

Miss Expatria

2003-05-15

They do not have a word here for "boo-boo,'" as in, "Baby has a boo-boo on her toe." "Boo-boo" is a part of "bu-bu, settete," which is like "peek-a-boo" for kids.

The first time I saw this in print I read it out loud, "bu-bu, sette tete," which means "peek-a-boo, seven tits," which of course gave me and my cleavage a new nickname I shall never live down.

2003-05-20

I sat behind an old couple on the bus last night; they were talking quietly, and all of a sudden he broke out in the softest, most beautiful tenor voice, singing to his wife.

Alan the Irish Guy works at the Internet place every day, like me. I think he does something highly suspect. I think he either works for M5, or he is a freelance anarchist. It is fun to speak English with him, though. He's always doing something with a band of crazy protester-type people, and they all smell. Is that a requirement? I need to write more about them because they are fascinating, but they are always sitting right next to me, being stinky.

Sometimes I feel like I am in the Hotel New Hampshire, minus the bear.

Sylvietta, the neighborhood cat, sleeps in the shade on the marble ledges of the buildings when it gets hot.

Miss Expatria

2003-05-22

We watched *San Remo* '94 and '97 on video, fast-forwarding through particularly bad singers. Vincenzo loves Ana Oxa, and she just… sucks. She sounds like a dead cat. But I love Giorgia, and they hate her. Giorgia seems to be like the Celine Dion of Italy, complete with sickeningly saccharine personal life, but her voice is gorgeous; but as I've said before, singing along with her is definitely the most satisfying way to learn Italian.

My personal favorite entry, from *San Remo* '97, was an all-white Italian reggae band, singing in a Veneto dialect about needing a black Pope since they already have a black Miss Italia. There was just too much to appreciate in that number.

There was some kind of mess with the buses the other day (surprise), and as we're sitting in ridiculous traffic, from behind me I hear, "Che *paaaaaaalle*" ("Oh, balls") in this total clenched-teeth Vanderbilt voice. I look behind me and there is this decked-out, pissed-off, elegant woman. She looked like it might have been the first time she was ever on public transportation. I wanted her to be my friend.

I am in love with this straight, hot florist in my neighborhood. He is so, so fine. This now brings the total to four men in my immediate neighborhood who are simply delicious in four completely different ways - along with the nice cool guy from the fan shop, who still owes me breakfast; the guy in the dry goods shop that's always playing jazz on a guitar; and the cheese guy, whose knowledge of cheese as well as his salt-and-pepper hair makes me swoon. It certainly makes running my errands a joy.

Of course, I get the creepy super of my building, the letchy restaurant owner in the piazza, and the mouth-breather fishmonger down the street lusting after me. It never fails.

Alan and the smelly anarchists are gone today, no doubt instilling terror in some unsuspecting world power somewhere. I would love to hang out with them; they seem like fun. But they smell.

2003-05-29

My mom told me last night that apparently, I am slated as a speaker at their Italian American club this summer when I come home for a visit. I have to speak about my experiences living in Rome. Since I am sure my life with the gay mafia is probably not an appropriate topic, I thought I would provide tips for the traveler:

- Tip #1 - Refrain from looking like a smacked ass at all times. This includes clothing and behavior.
- Tip #2 - Learn some basic Italian phrases and do not be scared to use them. It will get you far.
- Tip #3 - Keep your voice down. Y'all talk so loud.
- Tip #4 - Italians eat late and take all night. Copy them. You will have a better dining experience.
- Tip #5 - It's not a forced march. Slow down and look around you as you go from one must-see to the next. That's where life is.

Miss Expatria

2003-06-06

Some neighborhood thoughts:

Every night when I walk down to get my bus, I pass this little workshop. I first saw it in 2001, and the scene is the same every night I pass. There is an older Italian man who is either eating or working on some piece of something, like metal or something, and sitting silently in the corner is an African girl. There is also a dog in the doorway.

So one day I ask Marco what the deal is, and he tells me that the guy is a loan shark. Some other guy defaulted on his loan, and that's how he got the girl. He told me just like that, like he was telling me how to turn on my computer.

I love this restaurant near work, Taverna Romana - or as I like to call it, the Meatball Palace, as it is the only place I have been to so far that has meatballs on the menu, served as a main course. Sometimes if I'm flush I'll go there for lunch before work, by myself, with a book; if I'm too late, the old lady who runs it with an iron fist, whom I secretly call the Meatball Lady, meets me at the door and screams NO PASTA because they've already turned off the stove.

But if I get there early enough, I order either spaghetti carbonara or rigatoni cacio e pepe, with the meatballs - and the Meatball Lady's husband, who looks as though he has been hen-pecked since the earlier part of the 20th century, smiles and tells me he remembers that I want both dishes at the same time.

Then they watch in amazement as I eat the pasta and the meatballs simultaneously, sometimes IN THE SAME BITE. One time, they called a friend over from another table, and they stood over me and gazed in wonder.

Alice and Massimiliano are this couple who live up the street; they do not smell, but smelly anarchists live with them. Marco and I are both in love with both of them. They're just funky and fun and funny and stylish and cool. Yesterday when I was outside, Massimiliano came running out of the house shirtless and shoeless to get something out of his car. He said, "Ciao, bella" to me, but I can't remember if I said anything back because I almost passed out. He is sssssssso fine.

I picked up my laundry today and when I got home I found they had wrapped up their stapler in my packages, and I went and returned it to them. The wife seems really cool and nice but the guy, although he is always nice to me, seems like he probably has hit her before. And one morning, I smelled whisky on his breath.

When they take your clothes, they write out your name on tiny slips of paper and staple them to each piece of clothing, even underwear. I want to bring back from the States a huge roll of the numbered tickets for them. Think of what a revelation it would be!

2003-06-09

Today, I found the most fabulous pair of shoes in the window of a shoemaker's shop. They are black and silver sling backs with kitten heels. They were so cheap, I would say they were used but it's obvious no one had ever worn them. Maybe the lady never picked them up from him or something.

This shop is right across the street from my house (and here I am, searching far and wide for shoes). It is like a little cave, with a loft and about 500 wooden foot forms hanging from the ceiling. Like all the people I visit in their tiny shops, he chats with me about any old thing that pops into his head. I love him and want to put him in my pocket.

When you run the kinds of errands where you drop something off to be repaired or whatever, no one here ever gives you a ticket or even asks your name. They just tell you to check back on a certain day to see how they're coming along. They all have the sharpest minds.

I am wearing my big sunhat today and am very fetching.

2003-06-11

It's so hot, all I can do is laugh. Holy hell hot. And nothing has air conditioning.

I was waiting for the bus at Termini with like 100 other people, which was annoying because we were all smushed together under the shade of one asthmatic tree, when I noticed that the traffic out on the street was not moving at all. So I started walking, because who knows how long I could possibly stand there.

I get to the corner, and there is some sort of full-scale crazy arrest going on: Empty buses askew in the middle of the intersection, six police vans, and about two dozen men freaking out and resisting arrest and carrying a fake open coffin with plastic, crayon-colored flowers coming out of it. It was total chaos and no one knew what the hell was going on.

It was a pretty awesome spectacle.

I had to stop and gawk next to some ridiculous American girl who said to her friend, "Why are they arresting these poor men that are trying to bury their friend? Maybe he was a cop." Indignantly, like she was going to march off to the Human Rights Commission; like she couldn't believe we were witnessing this crime against humanity.

It was SO OBVIOUSLY a fake cardboard coffin, shaped like a big fake Dracula coffin, half spray-painted black, and only two people were carrying it, lazily, kind of swinging it around. And why would the cops be handling these men violently who were trying to bury a cop, anyway?

I said to her, as nice as I could, "No, it's a fake coffin," because I just couldn't take the blatant ignorance.

She looked at me like I had six heads. She says, indignant again, "Well, what's going on then?" And I say, "I'm not sure. My guess would be, some kind of protest." And she gives her friend a look like I am the ignorant one.

In other news, Vincenzo and Marco are making hilarious, vicious fun of a Mariah Carey song right now. They have been eating tomato and basil sandwiches all day, and the basil is from Vincenzo's terrace, and it smells so good, fresh, and sweet I am about to DIE RIGHT HERE.

2003-06-14

Rome broke a heat record Thursday. 35.8 Celsius. If you use my method of adding 16 and then doubling it, that's... so hot. Today is supposed to be 40.

My best friend for over 25 years, Kevin, actually showed up in my part of the world, for 24 hours, on his way to Milan for a meeting.

He is a big wig at a big pharma company. I find it hilarious that people think he's important and smart; I mean, he is, but when you've known somebody since they were six, it's hard to take them too seriously.

His secretary always answers his phone at work; I always say I'm Rosemary Hughes, or Kerry Larkin, or Julie McGonigle - girls we went to grammar school with. He always picks up the phone laughing.

We went to the place near my apartment that has only seafood on the weekends, and sat outside in the shade. We ate spaghetti and clams and split a mixed seafood plate. And a bottle of Frascati, the delicious white wine from up in the hills outside Rome.

Then ice cream with the gay mafia, who had to meet him. We stood outside Romalife, all of us eating as fast as we could before it all melted, and they tried out their combined knowledge of English on Kevin. He was thoroughly charmed.

Went back to my 'hood and stopped in at a bar to have a drink, where the already-drunk barman drank many drinks with us while telling us that Afghanistan, Iraq and Iran should all be A-bombed. I was translating for Kevin and he was trying not to crack up, because the guy was hammered and looked like he could become belligerent if he thought we were making fun of him.

Went to Trimani and had two more bottles of Frascati and little plates of yummy food. Came home very drunk, and passed out in front of the fan.

Love him to death. Thank you God, for my best friend.

I had to go into Romalife today as Marco had absconded with my bottle of Aleve, which he is now addicted to, and which I have to have because otherwise, the aspirin here gets dissolved in a glass like Alka-Seltzer, which is just gross. Marco spent the better part of a cigarette laughing at me and my hangover.

2003-06-16

I have spent the last two days in my underwear in front of my fan. We broke another heat record. They are telling children and old people to stay at home.

If this city had clothes dryers and/or air conditioners, it would be perfect. But it does not have these things, so it is deeply, deeply flawed. But I love it anyway.

Miss Expatria

The funniest thing I have ever read was in the paper yesterday. They said that all the air conditioners in use have caused random blackouts. Where would these be, exactly? Because if they mean the six air conditioners in existence in this entire province, they have big, big problems.

2003-06-17

My window faces onto a courtyard and I love laying around at all hours of the day and listening to people's lives:

--All the clanking dishes and silverware and conversations at lunchtime
--A mom and a tiny boy who, every day, come to serious blows; the boy sounds like a tiny Mussolini, laying out his argument in full-scale oratory
--My neighbors in their bathroom. The most annoying thing sounds like someone tapping a plastic vial against a marble counter to make the stuff in the vile settle. TAP TAP TAP TAP TAP, always five times a piece, and for about 20 minutes. I have no idea what this sound is and I like to imagine what it is they could possibly be doing. I hate repetitive sounds
--Every night at about midnight, the same phone rings twice. Insert postman joke of your choice
--All the phones in my courtyard's apartments are all old phones, with actual rings, very romantic
--People sometimes blast their music, but it is always cool music - so far I have heard opera, Bjork, The Cure, U2, and some really good Italian artists

--The couple next to me either fights or watches movies on what must be a tremendously advanced system. I always thought the girl sounded like a bitch, and then one day I saw her, and she looks like she'd be a bitch. I saw the guy one day and he had on an American Girl Scouts t-shirt
--When I water my plants, I stand and wait to hear the water crash four flights below

2003-06-19

The front door to the apartment building next to mine has a big pink ribbon on it. They do that for new babies, and I was ruminating on how moving and community-spirited it was until the baby screamed into the courtyard for nine hours last night. Then I realized the pink ribbon was in fact a warning sign for everyone else to RUN LIKE HELL.

2003-06-24

I dropped off my rent to Alessio, Hot Landlord. Normally I cannot speak at all because his hotness triggers a brain malfunction, but last night I was totally holding my own.

2003-06-25

Eleonora is screaming about a scorpion in the bathroom at Romalife. The scorpion is in there because I have drunk a lot of water today and have to pee every five minutes.

2003-07-01

It is really slow at the New York office today, and really slow here in the shop as well. Marco and I have been sitting outside on the stoop all this late, humid afternoon, catching breezes, watching the light change, petting passing dogs, talking about everything and nothing at all, swapping languages like baseball cards, and it was the light, sweet feeling of being alive that made me come back in and document this non-occasion.

And now time and the world has seemed to start up again: hot Massimiliano is here and eating something that smells yummy; the other Marco from upstairs stopped in to pick something up; another friend is here and cracking us up.

I love my life.

2003-07-02

I made pancakes and bacon for Marco and Vincenzo this morning; brought it into work and they devoured it. Despite my instructions and the forks and knives I helpfully brought in, they still ate them like tacos.

I went to the bookstore in Termini train station last night, which featured freezing cold jet blasts of air from the ducts underneath the shelves. Needless to say, I was an hour in there.

Wait, have I talked about this particular bookstore? It is basically an enormous glass box in the middle of the front room of Termini, across from where you buy your tickets.

The fiction is arranged by publisher, so it forces you to walk up and down every aisle. It's horrible when you know what you are looking for, but great for browsing.

Also, the shelves end at chest height and a lot of the books are laid out cover-up, another great thing for browsing (and people watching).

I'm working on moving away from books in Italian I have read previously in English to actual Italian books written by Italians. I don't think I'm ready yet. Instead, I got an Italian translation of an American book I've never read before. We'll see how it goes.

2003-07-03

Who did I see on my way to work but Alessio, Hot Landlord? I of course became completely flustered and with my inability to be flip and flirty in Italian, I think I came off... somewhere between sophomore and junior year of high school.

He is probably engaged.

2003-07-14

Friday night Marco, Eduardo (Marco's new boyfriend: Cute!) and I went to see *The Italian Job*. The best part was the air conditioning in the movie theater - the first true A/C coldness I have felt in Italy, ever.

Saturday, Marco, Eduardo, his two friends from Amsterdam, Marta and Susanna, and I all went to a free concert in Piazza del Popolo. Marta and Susanna are both from Portugal, but have England/Holland/several other countries between them; we all agreed we felt like a tiny UN contingent.

The crowd was amazingly well behaved. A great many of them had been there all day listening to other bands, and there was a lot of beer readily available. This combination anywhere else would have meant puking teenagers, fistfights and general rambunctiousness. But everyone at the concert was totally chilling out, texting in between numbers and generally paying attention.

We saw Craig David and Alanis Morrisette; they both gave really good performances. We sang along to "Thank U" using Vincenzo's lyrics - *Thank you Indians, Thank you Terrence* - and got strange looks from the people around us.

After, we went for the late night cornetto that I love love love. Not only are they so yummy and delectable; there are no tourists there, and it is always like 3AM when we go, and everyone is just completely focused on the yumminess.

We were walking through Villa Borghese on the way to the concert and across this huge piazza was one of the museums in the park, your typical, beautiful, classic building. It looks like Grand Central Terminal a little bit; or rather, Grand Central Terminal looks like it. Across the top of the museum in very white neon was the following phrase, in English, all in caps:

EVERYTHING IS GOING TO BE ALRIGHT

It stopped me in my tracks. I felt like it was there just for me. It moved me, in the quietest of ways, more than I can possibly explain. I haven't been able to get the image, or the emotion, out of my soul.

Miss Expatria

2003-07-15

Using a chopstick, string, and packing tape, I fixed the slats on my futon bed in one hour. I am MacGuyver.

I got minutes on my phone, so now I can call Alessio, Hot Landlord and tell him when I am leaving, and maybe flirt a bit. Although, he seems to find it charming when I cannot think of a word in Italian; maybe I will just try to speak normally and wait for my mind to blank out.

I like my little, crappy cell phone. And I love the idea of paying as you go for cell phone usage. There are no contracts, no hidden fees, no incomprehensible monthly bills. You pay, you talk. Brilliant! At home I think this would be considered pretty ghetto, but here, everyone does it.

2003-07-16

It is relentlessly, angrily hot here. Isn't there some kind of physics rule involved in it HAVING TO RAIN once the humidity reaches 100%? Shouldn't it just HAPPEN?

One week from today I will be whisked away to Paris on a swanky night train, and then get on a buddy-pass flight courtesy of my pilot cousin to the good old U. S. of A.

I'm really worried about passing through immigration on both sides - I never did find a way to live here legally. But, if the worst case scenario happens and they detain me or something, I think I have a pretty strong case - my job could not be done by an Italian, or anyone else for that matter; and I spend money here.

Giovanni asked me if I was excited to go to New York, as I will have to do for work when I get back. I thought about it - I am not. I want to see my friends, but the LAST thing I actually want to do is be in New York. I have a new city, and this city knows me well; it treats me kind, and I am in love with it.

Things I am not looking forward to:

- Morning commutes to my awful, depressing office
- Urine-saturated surfaces
- Loud people, loud city
- Housewives in SUVs
- People with an over-inflated sense of self-importance
- Self-consciously fashionable office girls who watch too much *Sex In The City*
- Pushing and shoving
- Unappealing architecture
- High prices
- Mean people
- Using an alarm clock to wake up

Things I am looking forward to:

- Ess-a-Bagel with whitefish salad
- Being treated to fabulous dinner by my food snobby friend Rich
- Burrito Bar brunch; entree and four frozen margaritas, $12.95

- Sleepovers at Katie's, and at MK's
- Long, decadent brunch at Yaffa's T Room
- Taking a taxi at the end of the night, and watching the city go by
- Indian lunch with gang from work
- Bullshitting with Frank the comptroller in his office, using the telescope I gave him to spy on rooftop sunbathers

2003-07-18

It is midday. The sky is a monochrome white. The sun is a bright orange ball. At any second, the peninsula on which I live will spontaneously burst into flames. It's HOT.

BIG NEWS: when I come back after my trip, I will be living in a new place with Marco and someone else!

We moved my stuff into the new apartment, and it is amazing. It doesn't have anything in it right now; they just laid down all new tiles (and this is Italy, so I mean stone), and all the bulbs are bare.

My room is lovely, with large doors leading onto the terrace that connects my room with Marco's room. The doors have wooden shutters on the inside and the normal metal, slatted shutters on the outside.

Gabe, part owner of the apartment and the only American I know here, told me that I have absolutely nothing to worry about regarding going home. I can very easily lie and say I had been with a tour group, and they never stamped my passport. He is also illegal here. He is with Francesca, whose sister is Marco's ex-boyfriend's employee, which is how we got the apartment.

We went to a place in our new neighborhood that was delish. I had a crepe with Gorgonzola and walnuts, and a salad with braesola and Parmigiano. YUM. We all had two courses and lots of wine and we each paid 13.50 euro. Our new neighborhood is packed with cool, cheap restaurants and bars.

There is a common misconception about Italy that one can sit at a cafe all day and chill, like one can in France. First of all, there are not really cafes here; they are all bars. Secondly, while one can find bars with outdoor seating, most bars are empty inside save an actual bar, cashier's desk, and maybe a video gambling machine. Italians mostly pop in, slam down an espresso, maybe talk for five minutes, and leave. They do not hang out in bars; they save the hanging out for meals.

Chapter Seven

2003-07-27

Wednesday was hot, hotter than hot. I got on the overnight train to Paris and they had not turned on the AC yet, and it was ridiculously awfully close and stuffy, like an attic. The lady with whom I was sharing the tinsy, bunk-bed room brought - blessed treasure! - a TINY CHILD. And two huge bags. This was not going to work.

I corralled the conductor and asked her as nicely as I could if there were any free beds in another two-bedder, so that the mother and child reunion could have more space. She said she would see what she could do and gave me a glass of prosecco. The train started up and the poorest excuse for A/C came out of the vents. I have never been so drenched in sweat in my life.

Miraculously, in the confusion surrounding a fat American couple complaining about the size of their beds, she scooped me up and deposited me into my very own room. She is My Fourth Italian.

I stripped off my dripping clothes, put on my nightgown, cranked up the A/C, opened the window and locked the door. I was in for the night, and no one was going to move me from my new kingdom.

Miss Expatria

I slept fitfully on the tiny sofa until the room cooled down enough that I could climb into the loft bed. I have always slept like the dead on trains, and this time was no exception. I woke up at 8:30 and McGuyvered my way around there being no water in our car, got dressed, and watched France wake up out my window as I ate a croissant and drank hot chocolate, generously brought to me by my fairy godmother, the conductor.

Arrived in Paris and dream of dreams! It is cool and rainy! I never thought I would be so happy to see shitty weather. My hotel room is adorbs: Huge tub, chenille bedspread, and balcony overlooking rue Victoria.

It is only about 11:30AM; I have been to Paris several times before; it is raining; and I smell pretty ripe. This rare alignment of the planets means that I can play in the bath for a while, file my nails, watch CNN and generally luxuriate before tooling around Paris, visiting some of my favorite paintings and searching out dinner.

I am hoping that soaking in the tub also will alleviate the pain I have from falling down a flight of marble steps while moving out of my apartment; I bounced down on my tailbone and it is very sore and bruised. Luckily, Alessio, Hot Landlord had already left, and so did not witness this Lucille Ball moment.

§

Thursday, bed time. I did all my favorite Paris things today! Walked through the courtyards of the Louvre; went to the Musee D'Orsay; ate a crocque madame and pate de campagne (no foie gras at the place I chose, but the pate de campagne was so garlicky and the bread was so fresh); watched the sunset from the Pont Neuf. It is 10PM and still quite light here.

I am not fully here; I am half in Rome and half in OC. I will wake up a week from now and laugh thinking of this perfect day; but I know even as I went through this day, I was not looking at what I was seeing.

Paris cannot compare to that which I now call my home. I have always had a crush on Paris; but when I went through my horrible, lengthy breakup with New York, I ran not to my crush, but to the one I always secretly knew was for me - Rome. I belong there, and coming here has made it even more apparent. It takes a quiet, mighty love to not feel anything in the face of your crush. Rome is it.

Tomorrow I will be awakened by a horribly expensive and completely necessary breakfast served in my room. I have arranged for transportation to the airport, and hopefully everything will go smoothly with the check-in and Immigration.

I have changed more in this last year than I could ever conceive possible. I am emotionally and physically leaner; I speak two languages; I have an apparently endless supply of personal strength. It will be fascinating to see if anyone else sees these changes.

What will happen next?

§

Miss Expatria

Friday night, Paris. Wow, did today suck.

Got to the airport. Confirmed listing. Was randomly chosen to go through extensive security searches. Survived passport control. Did not get on plane - all booked. Little consolation were the dozen other people also stranded here.

After much back and forth in my head, opted NOT to go back into Paris, but am at Ibis hotel at the airport. Shitty food; have just watched a snake give birth and a spider eat a cricket on TV. Also saw a horrible show called *Dismissed* on MTV that made me fear for the next generation, but it was dubbed in German so I might be misinterpreting it.

Am booked on flights tomorrow from here to Chicago and Chicago to Philly. We shall see. If I keep getting kicked off of flights I am going to need more money, or I will have to sleep in the airport.

My phone is out of minutes; my computer is about to be out of battery; I left my remaining bubble bath and powder in Paris.

Apparently this is my penance for having a perfect day yesterday.

§

Saturday: I knew I wasn't getting on that plane. Shit.

Miss Expatria

Email from Marco, which he wrote in his best English:

Ciao Honey!

Maybe it's banal to say that I miss you so much. Everyday I see your empty work-emplacement, and I feel a sense of empty uselessness, and I start to cry, to roll in the floor and to thread a knife to me in the chest!

It's so hard my life in Romalife without my Christine, without our cigarettes, but above all without your lighter! The green one that you left me, it's died.

But it's more appropriate to say that there's no life without you in Romalife. So... For August I've changed the name of my store in "Roma e basta!!"

§

Sunday. Yes, Sunday, and I am still in Paris. This is my third check-in to the decidedly unglamorous Ibis Roissy-Ville. My mom is faxing her credit card info so I can stay. I have around 5 euro left on me.

I feel like this is the wait for the last helicopter out of Vietnam.

I found out the reason why I keep getting searched and frisked and stickered is I only have carry-on luggage. As a twist today, one guy asked me if I was carrying any jewels. I laughed out loud and said I was too poor for jewels, which made him laugh. But he meant jewelry, and I have a

Zip-Loc bag with some stuff. So that was a full dump of my suitcase.

I have had my passport stamped like 16 times from going back and forth through passport control. This strikes me as very, very funny, given my now-unfounded fear of being caught as an illegal immigrant.

I miss expressing myself in Italian, and I think I will miss that a lot at home. It was something I was so worried about moving to Rome, and I did not realize until I left that I really am able to express myself. The thing is though, it is not a literal translation of the way I would express myself in English. I am a different person in Italian, with a different sense of humor, and I use a different play on words.

§

Tuesday.

I have always gotten through my life with the saying, "Everything happens for a reason." I CANNOT WAIT to see the reason for THIS. I feel like I'm part of a game, but no one told me the rules - like I'm supposed to present some kind of code word or magic key at the check-in desk.

I heard last night on BBC news that the French have officially changed from the word "email" to some other French word. This should certainly further endear them to Americans. Also, if any ad here is in English, there is always an asterisk and a French translation is printed somewhere on the ad.

Miss Expatria

None of this bothers me personally; but when something is translated into English, it is done grudgingly in bad English. This succeeds in making them look rather uneducated to me instead of triumphantly French. If you are going to provide a translation, at least do it the best you can.

I am doing pretty well overall, and my days have already fallen into a pattern. I am by no means amused by my circumstances, but I have adapted. It calms me to think that I COULD be doing this with Pavlov Memento, who would have been absolutely insufferable.

Email from Marco:

Carissima!!! I'm so sorry for your disguise! I can imagine that you are so sad and SCOGLIONATED!

May I help you in any way? Please tell me if there's a possible way! I should be happy to help you! I gave your e-mail address to Edoardo, too... So he will write to you and maybe he will give you some confort.

I've checked the part in english of my mail of last morning, and I've found a lot of errors! Could you ever forgive me?

Oh... In this moment a black man is seated on your chair... What a strange sensation...

Ok fantastic Christine; now it's the time to cry in the bathroom... Maybe you're asking me: "why?"

*For your absence, obvious! (what a question!!) Sigh sigh...
...sob sob... ...sniff sniff...*

*I wait for (good, goodissime) news, so take care dolcissima
principessa!*

§

WEDNESDAY. Am going back to Rome tomorrow. Am
flying from Rome to the States with an ACTUAL TICKET
on 8/7.

This came about through a ton of finagling on Expedia.com
and the unbelievable generosity of my parents. Actually, I
bought four tickets - one round trip now, one round trip in
October for a wedding (not mine) - all as one multi-
destination trip, and got a spectacular price. Go figure.

§

Thursday, Bercy train station, Paris. My pay came through,
hurray! I found a pair of shoes while trekking around Paris.
Only 20 euro! Baby blue and beaded and FABULOUS.

Just had Indian lunch - um, they had BEEF on the menu.
Of course I had it, because when will I ever again see beef
on an Indian menu? Nothing was really spicy; I guess they
are catering to the French palate. I did have gulab jamun,
however, and it was lovely. I spoke French to the waiter
and slipped into Italian; he thought it was Spanish and
started speaking Spanish to me; we both became very
confused and when I told him I was American, he gave up
entirely and walked away in a huff.

Miss Expatria

2003-08-02

I got the compartment to myself on the way back to Rome; my steward was totally a hottie, he found hot chocolate for me in the morning. As I sat there in my nightgown drinking the hot chocolate and smoking a French cigarette, I watched a crystal-clear rainbow appear against a rolling black sky and then disappear into Tuscan hills. And I laughed.

Yesterday I worked, and then Vincenzo and I went shopping for dinner. I'm staying at his place, along with Marco; we're both homeless until September, when our apartment is ready.

On the way we had to stop at his favorite public fountain to fill up a bottle with what he insists is the best water in Rome. Everyone here has their favorite fountain, and everyone insists their fountain has the best water.

We went home and made chicken cutlets and a salad with lettuce, finocchio, apples and corn. We ate on V's terrace, with Christmas lights and candles. It was nice; cool breezes and lovely.

2003-08-06

I met Viola! She is our new roommate, and now one of three girls I know in Rome.

She speaks faster than anyone on the planet, so I came off retarded since I was about 10 seconds behind her in comprehension. She is a little shorter than me, and is chunky, curvy, like me, and she too has lost a lot of weight recently; how weird is that? She seems really nice; once I get used to her way of speaking, I think we will get along just fine.

Marco treated me to lunch today and he will treat for dinner tonight, since I have 5 euro left and do not want to take out 50 right before I leave. YAY for best friends! He told me that this morning for breakfast he made scrambled eggs with pancake syrup, and he thinks it will become his new vice.

In other news, Rome might burst into flames AT ANY SECOND since it is hotter than ACTUAL HELL.

Chapter Eight

I spent a month at home, seeing family in Ocean City and working a bit in New York, crashing with friends there. I went through reverse culture shock, which was very embarrassing – what can be more tedious than someone who grew up in America but swoons over a glass filled with ice and constantly points out how big the cars are?

The most startling change was inside myself. I knew I had changed a lot, but I had no idea how much until I was back home. My life had slowed down; I had lost about 30 pounds; I listened more, and spoke less, around family, friends and colleagues; I actually FORGOT ENGLISH WORDS, like a true expat asshole.

But more than that, I just could not relate to the things they were talking about, or get excited about the things that made them excited. It just wasn't me anymore.

I had no words for what I had been through and discovered; I could present no reference for how I now lived. I wound up smiling and nodding a lot.

Don't get me wrong: I was not miserable being back in the States. My family is amazing, supportive and my true

Miss Expatria

inspiration, and I loved every second I spent with them. I loved seeing my beach, my ocean; I loved sleeping in my bed in my old room, with the sea breeze as my air conditioner. My friends have known me for about a thousand years combined, and it was bliss being able to use all the references and memories we share without having to explain everything. There was no one who thought Joni Mitchell's album is called *The Hissing of Summer Lawyers*.

But in the year I had lived in Italy, I had completely assimilated into Italian culture – sometimes going days without uttering a single English word – and that will change anyone. As much as I loved seeing my family and friends, I really just wished they all had come to see me instead.

I could have shown them a great time.

Chapter Nine

2003-09-05

I'm back.

I have been speaking well since my return, but have been more stressed about it than before. I feel like Italian is coming out of my mouth within an inch of its life. I often have dreams where I have to do things I don't know how to do, or have forgotten, and I have to act like I know what I am doing. That is fine for a dream, despite all its symbolism; but I feel like that now, in real life, going about my daily business and it's highly unnerving.

I can tune out Italian really easily if I want, and I tend to do this when, for example, we are in the car and Vincenzo and Marco are bullshitting. I kind of like it because it makes me feel like when I was a little kid, in the backseat, listening to my parents talking, and I know everything is OK. But sometimes I miss out on stuff and my gay mafia gets mad at me. I have to be better about this.

Last night after work, Marco took me over to Luca's; Alfio was at work. There was Luca in their fabulous apartment, sitting cross-legged on the sofa, so glamorous and handsome and wise and brilliantly creative.

He asked me about American politics; he made fun of the American television he has seen on his new satellite TV ("It's all Paris Hilton and plastic surgery"); he told me a devastating tale of his friend Franca, and how their friendship has changed in the saddest way; he played videos of the songs he has written and produced; he showed me slide shows on his computer; he made us tea; he played with Tomas, the cat.

He is an icon to me. I want to build a shrine to him. It's like going to visit a holy man on a mountain who dispenses unconditional love and wisdom, and blesses you and sends you on your way.

2003-09-08

Sunday I made THE FIRST BRUNCH in our new place, which Marco, Viola and Giovanni ate with great abandon. Then we set to work on CASA NOSTRA, putting up lampshades and reorganizing drawers and pausing to smoke cigs on our balcony.

Luca and Alfio came over and we proudly showed off our work. Marco made pasta with artichokes and something else in it, and we sat around and bullshitted for a while. I tuned out a lot of what they were saying; I was exhausted because they were all talking at once and the music was playing and it was too much for my DELICATE EARS to handle.

Miss Expatria

2003-09-10

This is why I like it here:

Today I had 6 euro on me, and I bought:

Lunch
Large bottle of water
Cigarettes
Bus ticket

A lady who lives across the street apparently bought a new synthesizer, because last night she tested every single feature on it well into the early hours. Luckily, she actually knows how to play stuff on it - I heard Rhapsody in Blue on trumpets, harpsichord, strings and robot voice.

I texted Marco: MA CHE CAZZO E QUESTA MUSICA

He wrote back: OH, I DON'T KNOW - MEET YOU ON THE BALCONY

This happens often - not texting from room to room, but me speaking in Italian and Marco speaking in English. We did not notice that we do it until someone else pointed it out to us recently.

And so we met on our balcony from our rooms, and we together stared at the lady in her window and yelled insults. She was oblivious. There must have been six other people hanging out their windows, all yelling at her.

Miss Expatria

Earlier, Marco made a salad consisting of:

Lettuce
Hard-boiled eggs
Peaches
Cheese
Carrots
Pancake syrup
Balsamic vinegar
Olive oil

...AND IT ROCKED. Go figure.

2003-09-12

I was thinking of New York yesterday, all day. It's like an ex-lover, and yesterday was the anniversary of our break-up, so all day I think about how great and idyllic it was before the break-up, but then the break-up was so horrible; it wasn't anyone's fault really, it wasn't personal, but after the break-up there was just no going back to like it was before.

I miss New York like I'd miss a lover. It knows I was there last month; it was smiling smugly at me, knowing I would come back under false pretenses ("I had to work and see my friends"); it knew I was there because at one time, it was the only love in my life.

But now I have a new love, and this love is quieter, more beautiful, more mature. I take my time with this love; it holds me tenderly and delights me with surprises every day. But I know this love cannot last; it is too sweet, too exotic.

And where else will I go, what will I turn to, when this affair ends? I know it, bitterly. I know I will go back to the one that stole my heart, who swept me off my feet and gave me the strength I needed to eventually leave it.

2003-09-15

This neighborhood just gets better and better. Guess what I found around the corner from my house? A creperie. I got two crepes - one with artichokes and cheese, and another with Gorgonzola, marscapone and walnuts. Holy shit, were they good.

Vincenzo came about 6ish with Enzo from Naples and a WASHING MACHINE! ...that fell off the back of a truck, if you know what I mean. It was like 50 bucks, or something ridiculous. In between everything else Marco was doing (making dough and hanging my curtains and putting up hooks and drilling and spackling) he helped them hook it up, and I did a wash!

It is in our bizarrely long and narrow bathroom. Of course the light went crazy as soon as they got it in there (think disco strobe light), so I gave them a flashlight and it was Vince, Marco and Enzo all crowded around the washer, talking incessantly and pointing and chatting and doing light tricks with the flashlight. We all crowded around and watched the first cycle start. It was like having the first TV in the neighborhood.

The pizza was great, but poor Marco was in the kitchen the whole time. He made a couple of margarita pizzas, one with sausage and sauteed mushrooms, one with three cheeses and black pepper, and one with rucola, mozzarella and tomatoes. Alfio brought tiramisu.

Marco did not seem to mind that he had been working on this meal, among 10,000 other things, since like 10AM. I just do not have patience for that kind of cooking. I told him: If I can't prepare it while the water is boiling, I don't make it.

2003-09-16

OK, I have officially become annoyed with something Italian: The washing machines.

They are just different - they take two to three hours to cycle through, and they have no dryers, and it's just annoying. It has taken me three days to do four loads of laundry. And now there are clothes on the stendino (drying rack) and all over the house, not really drying. Thank God the crazy wet scirocco wind hasn't hit yet; I'd be naked.

In other news – in a fugue state of cocktail craving and language miscommunication, Marco and I have wound up with an enormous bottle of bitters. What the hell am I supposed to do with this enormous bottle of bitters?

2003-09-18

I made a sausage and meat gravy all day, and Giovanni and Marco are going to have it tonight. I am so nervous I can barely function. It is the first non-brunch thing I have made, and not only that, it is Italian. I am freaking.

2003-09-19

They loved it. THEY. LOVED. IT.

They were so cute: Marco and Gio hovering around the kitchen, sniffing at the pot, making sure I cooked the pasta correctly.

I wanted to make a full pound (half kilo) of rigatoni, so maybe I could have some left over, and they were SCANDALIZED. I told them that a) I made a lot of gravy and b) my parents and I eat a pound. Further scandalization ensued.

Twenty minutes later all the pasta was gone, and they both had bread in the serving bowl, scooping up the extra sauce. BUONISSIMO, they kept saying.

I have never been so proud in my whole life. I called my mom and everything.

This morning I reorganized all the shelves in the kitchen, scoured the sink and stove, mopped my room, dusted, and then did laundry. If I do not get my period soon, our house will be positively sterilized.

I might even try to cook again.

2003-09-20

Last night Marco made a frittata with potatoes and rosemary, and pasta with broccoli romana, which is leafy, ass-tasting crap. I tried to like it - he cooked it well - but in the end it was too vegetabley for me. The pasta was awesome, though.

Luca and Alfio brought over another couple, two huge, beefy men: One a Carabinieri, and the other a polizia who also does ballroom dancing. They were very funny, and they liked the peanut butter and apples I made them try.

And then Marco had a Nutella sandwich, which I did not have any of because I wanted to savor the garlic taste in my mouth for a little while longer. Then we went out on our balcony with our little folding chairs and smoked cigarettes and giggled and made fun of people walking by. He is the best girlfriend EVER.

2003-09-22

Salvatore and the three Vincenzos came over for dinner. Marco made a vegetable tart thing with Gorgonzola. Then he made rigatoni with radicchio and speck and other cheesy products and cream. THEN he made this dessert with sugared ladyfinger things in peach syrup with amoretto and fresh whipped cream and peaches and Nutella.

So, you know, dinner sucked as ususal.

2003-09-23

We have been having lizards in Romalife for the last two days. They are amusing. I just hope one does not crawl up my leg.

Miss Expatria

2003-09-25

Last night, I went to see this woman Nicolette who is from my hometown and is here with a tour group. My dad gave her my mail and I went to pick it up from her. I met her once before and she is a really nice lady. I gave her my number in case she needs anything while she's here.

This morning she calls me: Her tour company WENT BANKRUPT, so their tour is over before it has even begun. Those bastards got them all to Italy and then told them the tour was over, so they did not have to refund the $4000 (!!) each of the 35 people paid.

She told me one horror story after another - of a woman who saved for three years to pay for the tour, and was planning on only eating the pre-planned meals and scrimping any way she can. Of the couple who was going to be married while on the tour, in Venice. Of the married couple that had saved for two years to take their dream vacation in Italy before they start having kids.

I took Nicolette to dinner - it was the least I could do. She has done so many things in her life! We talked a bunch and walked all over. We ate at the Meatball Palace and she loved it. She insisted on paying, so I took her for ice cream and then a drink at the roof garden at her hotel, which is one of the highest points in Rome. The old waiter up there was delighted that I spoke Italian and quizzed me on all the sites we could see, and told me I could come back and have a drink as his guest whenever I pleased.

Miss Expatria

I took a taxi home and while waiting in the queue, everyone watched four American twits run screaming through the Termini bus lot, trying to stop cabs from circling around to get us in the queue. They thought they were being sexy and raucous, but in fact they were slutty and obnoxious.

Today there was an American girl and her mom on the bus, listening to a Chinese woman talking on her cell in the back of the bus. The girl says, loudly, WHAT AN UGLY LANGUAGE. Then she proceeded to name all the other UGLY LANGUAGES she could think of. Then the mom says, THAT GUY SMELLS DISGUSTING, WHY CAN'T THEY WASH.

Then two American girls got on and loudly complained how hot the city was today (about 70 and sunny) and how freezing it will be here in November (not a chance, girls).

Come on, you guys. We already have a bad reputation worldwide for being ignorant and loud. Get it together, OK?

Chapter Ten

2003-09-29

Vincenzo picked me up at 7:45 and our first stop was Therme Dicleblahblahblah, I have no idea what that second word is even though I pass the thing every single day. It's all part of Notte Bianca - every site in Rome is open all through the night until 7PM tomorrow. And everything is free.

We found great parking right off Piazza della Reppublica in an empty little lot, and we had a guided tour of the epigraphy exhibit at Therme Dicleblahblahblah. Sometimes I tuned out and walked around and looked at stuff, but it was fascinating. One of the sarcophagi was for the man who was the director of the gladiator games! How cool is that?

When we left, we went into the bath halls themselves and there were these intense exhibits: One involving enormous slide shows akin to *Clockwork Orange*'s inoculation scene, with ominous sounds lurking about, and another one with huge slabs of ice and pots with fire and more weird sounds being pumped in from God only knows where. The enormous, cavernous halls were basically pitch black, except for the light from the slide shows and pots of fire.

When we left there we were absolutely stunned to see that everything was packed - traffic jams, hordes of people everywhere. I have never seen so many people in one place who were not protesting something.

We were late for our next reservation at Domus Aurea, Nero's underground palace, so we took a packed, hot train over to find we had lost our reservation completely. So we walked back, sat in the car, and ate some of the food we had brought for a picnic. I cut up salami and cheese and white pizza bread, and we had olives. Vincenzo brought his mother's wine, and we sat and watched the crush of humanity in front of us and toasted every packed bus that lumbered past.

Then we took the rest of our food and walked up to Villa Borghese, for which we didn't need a reservation. The villa had amazing, enormous pictures illuminated onto the facade. By this time it's around 1AM – again, the crowds were tremendous and more people were flooding into the park every minute. We decided it would not be worth peering over people's shoulders. We found a place in the otherwise-empty park with a view of the Villa, lit some candles, spread out the tablecloth, and had a very civilized dinner al fresco. I made tortellini with thyme and basil, and he made baked tomatoes stuffed with rice and potatoes, and we finished the wine. Then we spread out on the blanket and watched people coming up the paths and looked up at the sky through the trees.

When we left there it was about 2:45 and there were still people streaming in; just as we got back to the car, it started to rain a bit.

I love that I can keep my huge French doors open and kind of close my shutters and let my curtains do a little of the billowing they do so well, and listen to the rain. It hasn't really rained like this in so long, SO LONG, and it is such a rich, sensuous sound. I want to stay up all night and listen to it. I think I will.

My life is filled with a constant stream of tiny luxuries that make every day perfect. What a gift my precious life is.

§

Sunday, 12:30PM - all the church bells in the city are ringing to let us know the lights are back on.

As soon as I got in bed, after Vincenzo dropped me off last night, the lights went off. Everywhere. I wrote the entry above and crashed out.

I woke up around 10AM and SMS'd my mom to watch the news and tell me what is going on. She told me that it apparently was a black out in all of Italy, and they are blaming France! I love it. When in doubt, blame France.

I was too excited by the implications of all of this, so I went out and bought pastries and cigarettes, and chatted with a group of old men who seemed to be the only ones around who were as excited as I was.

I ate half the pastries and smoked and impatiently waited for Marco to wake up, staring at his bedroom door and using telepathic brain waves. Marco finally got up and we ate the rest of the pastries and smoked on the balcony and talked. No work! Billions lost! People stuck on the metro! Deaths! Panic! Stinky people! And then the lights came back on and the church bells rang everywhere and now life is back to normal.

We snuck into Viola's room to watch the news (she is in Pisa) and there was only one station with any kind of coverage, which consisted of a man and woman in the studio who looked like they really did get dressed in the dark, and many shots of dark streets in Milan, Naples and other places.

Marco is going out to buy the paper (I think he thinks they will have news about this, but it only happened nine hours ago and in the middle of the night), and more pastries, and we will no doubt be in a diabetic coma by the time he gets around to making me the tagliolini he promised me.

"Black out" in Italian is "black out", but pronounced "blohckaauuuut".

§

Sunday, 11:23PM - Marco and I have decided to stop eating for the day. This would be a good thing. Tomorrow we vow to fast until we have kebab after work.

In other news…

Miss Expatria

Fabulous Ex-Boss Orlann is in fact coming in from Florence on Thursday, and will fly out Saturday morning. She said she wants to take taxis everywhere and she is paying for everything we do. She just wants to kind of whisk by all the sites, and then spend a lot of time drinking. I say, bring it on.

Orlann is a hilarious mixture of Patsy and Eddie from *Absolutely Fabulous*. She grew up in Portugal and South Africa, speaks three or four languages and has this *AbFab* accent, and although the most offensive, insulting things pop out of her mouth on a daily basis, I love her. And she loves me to death; she always says I am the smartest person she knows and she is enamored of my cleavage. Oh, and she told me that when I get sick of living here I can work for her at her new place and she will dump money on me. What more does one want in a Fabulous Ex-Boss?

2003-10-04

What a fabulous time I had with Fabulous Ex-Boss Orlann.

She took quite well to the city and walked around for hours; then we went back to my neighborhood and ate and drank at Vinarium, just down the street. All the walls are lined with wine bottles empty and full, the empty ones with candles in them, and big arched ceilings. It was ridiculously expensive for Rome but she was paying so, you know, cheers. When she was telling me about her super-elegant vacation in Tuscany with Famous Jimmy, she said, "We went to a wine farm." AWESOME.

Miss Expatria

Friday we went to the Vatican, and she really loved it. We went into one of the chapels there that is exclusively for praying. We knelt down and I was saying a prayer when I feel her nudge me. She says, in her fabulous accent, "That priest is hawwt, no?" We had to leave after that because I was sure lightning would strike us any minute. She also loved all the dead popes on display, and we discussed what they should do with this Pope when he dies.

She told me her current client is a pizza store chain that makes pizzas for working moms to take home and bake. This is funny, seeing as how she is neither a mother nor an eater. You know in *AbFab* when Patsy rubs her stomach in pain and Eddie asks her if she ate something, and Patsy says, "No, not since 1973?" That's Orlann.

Then we went to the Spanish Steps and walked down via Condotti and went into all the swanky stores and discussed fashion for two straight hours. We stopped into a bar where I mistakenly order fish juice (succo de pesce) instead of peach juice (succo de pesca). One vowel does a fool make.

Orlann and I bought wine and cheese and grapes and bread and pastries; Marco made cavatelli with zucchini, ricotta and speck; Viola made a potato and onion baked yummy thing; and Edo brought more wine. We ate and drank everything. Orlann ate everything she was served, which definitely goes down in the annals of history.

Viola was totally busting out her English; she was so proud, but I was in SHOCK because she NEVER speaks English to ME! We went to bed after the neighbors came and yelled at us for being too loud, because at 1:15AM we were not only still awake, but also causing a huge ruckus while the five of us attempted to shoo a lizard out of the living room.

This morning I saw her safely onto the train to Fiumicino. She is now off to London to meet back up with Famous Jimmy and they are going to Nobu and the theater etc., you can surely fill in the rest of their fabulousness.

Last night we were in my room and she repacked:

5 pairs of Prada shoes, all black
1 Comme de Garcon full-length winter coat, black
3 Versace dresses, all black
2 Pucci bandana shirts, Pucci colors
2 pairs Chanel sunglasses, black
1,498 other tiny pieces of designer clothing, all black

2003-10-06

Marco and I spent the night at home together hanging out, wearing pillows as hats, smoking cigarettes, and eating and drinking. I taught him "U-G-L-Y you ain't got no alibi, you ugly," and he spent about an hour trying to say it in the right cadence, failing miserably.

I finally have gotten my gay mafia into the habit of drinking the wine from larger glasses. We don't even try to be demure anymore; we just fill them up and drink away. Really, how annoying is it to pour wine 62 times into tiny cutesy glasses, when you all know you're going to keep drinking til the bottles are gone?

Chapter Eleven

2003-10-07

A year ago today, I started this life…

This is where my one-year anniversary journal entry was written.

I never thought I could be so happy. I never thought my days could be so carefree. And I never thought I would see a day when my life would be so fulfilled by the tiny, magical things that happen when you are in the right place, at the right time, with the right people.

And then, the rest of my life happened.

Chapter Twelve

2003-10-30

The chill in the air these days is reminding me of when I first moved here. When I look back into my memory and watch myself in my palazzo in Lavinio, I can't believe what I did with my life and I want to reach back through time and hug me and thank me.

I was rattling around in those empty cold rooms, writing Pavlov Memento out of my life in the journal Cynthia gave me, performing ruinous cooking experiments, sitting on one of my three balconies smoking cigs and staring at the sea, making elaborate tin foil mobiles to scare away pigeons, going slowly insane from the constant, screaming scirocco winds from Africa, taking long walks, waiting for my clothes to dry, and finding out who the hell I wanted to be.

The stifling trains; the sickening buses; the sad craziness of Hank's world; the Signora's watchful gaze; the weekly market; the first time a stranger said, "Ciao bella" to me; the hieroglyphics of a foreign washing machine; the eruption of the neighborhood when a goal was scored on TV; the layers of clothes I wore to bed every night; the shame of messing up the ordering procedure at the bar; the pride of doing everything myself; the daily ride along the sea and through the countryside; the smell of burning leaves.

It was hard as hell and absolutely wonderful and looking back, it was exactly what I needed.

My life is less of an adventure now, and more of a continuous great time.

Thinking of you, Lavinio, and wondering how you are - and glad I am not there.

2003-11-03

A year ago today, Pavlov Memento left the country after a failed month-long, half-hearted attempt to get me back. After he said goodbye, I sat in my palazzo and cried for about 40 straight hours at the finality of it. While I lived there, the only time I ever heard the nextdoor neighbors' dog was when he howled right along with me that whole weekend. I thought I might never stop crying, but you know what? I did.

Chapter Thirteen

2003-11-30

Jax came over for her birthday!

I took her for drinks at Tazio over at the Exedra Hotel, a swanky place that none of my broke gay mafia wants to go to. We were looking at the drinks menu when the waiter appeared from nowhere and served us two glasses of champagne with strawberries! We also got a plate of cichetti, which is called tapas in Spanish, which I think is what we call it in America - cold chicken with pate on top, tiny cold frittate, and an eggplant thing with rice and shrimp. It was awesome and we felt very glamorous.

Then we met Gio and Marco and went to Piccolo Abruzzo. The place was packed and HOT ALESSANDRO - not to be confused with Alessio, Hot Ex-Landlord - was presiding as always, holding our table right next to where he brings out the huge pans and serves up all the dishes. Much kissing and bellissima-ing all around.

As soon as we got situated, out came the food. I am going to list it all, because it was just so much:

- Risotto with broccoli stems and capers
- A plate of salami
- A plate of fresh mozzerella
- A plate of some kind of mortadella
- Steamed cabbage with bleu cheese, carrots and celery
- A plate of fresh ricotta
- Polenta exactly like my Aunt Dot's
- Papardella with rabbit sauce
- Bucatini all'amatriciana
- Penne arrabiata (at this point we were pleading for mercy, but to encourage us to eat, HOT ALESSANDRO and his sister Barbara came out from the kitchen and sat with us and ate, and HOT ALESSANDRO brought out more wine, and for every sip he took, we toasted Jackie)
- Four bottles of wine (not including the above)

Then the lights were turned off, the music was turned up, and HOT ALESSANDRO came out with a candle on top of something unidentifiable in the dark. Everyone cheered and Jax blew out the candle, and when the lights came back on, it was a mountain of profiteroles!

He served it up to the whole place, and it was quite possibly the best dessert I have ever had.

Then Barbara brought down four bottles of liqueur from the shelves that line the restaurant and parked them on our table for us to try, and HOT ALESSANDRO brought over the enormous jar of homemade biscotti. Jax put it directly on her lap and ate whatever was left in the jar. It was pure gluttony, and we waddled all the way home.

More notes from Jax's visit:

The President's Butcher - In her travels, Jax found a butcher with an 8-kilo turkey in the window, and it was ours on Saturday for a late Thanksgiving feast! The butcher cuts all the meat for President Ciampi, and was quoted on the front page of the New York Times regarding mad cow disease; he had the article proudly hanging next to a display counter filled with meat. He said he told the journalist who interviewed him a bunch of horrible things about BOOOSH, and asked us why they did not print them.

Aricia Pork Fest – We went to one of the hills outside Rome and chowed down on fresh roasted pork, salamis, cheeses, olives, bread, and homemade wine. It rocked. You walk up to these stands and order your food, then bring it into one of the taverns there that serves you their wine and gives you plastic plates to eat the food you've brought. It's not even a festival - it's like that all the time!

Thanksgiving Dinner - We did it! We did it! Nine people!! We made a turkey in a butter herb dressing, Stove Top stuffing FedExed from home, dirty mashed, sauteed sweet onions, string beans with almonds, cranberry sauce, salad, pumpkin pie, and chocolate cake. It took us days to find everything. They were terrified, poor things, to have everything on the same plate. But they got the hang of it and we had NO LEFTOVERS!! They loved the Stove Top stuffing and the Duncan Hines cake the best, which I find hilarious.

2003-12-09

Hey Jax -

So Viola decided to come to Naples with us after having some sort of bizarre discussion with Vincenzo on Thursday night about how she thought he didn't want her to come. We drove down Friday night after work and I got my first real taste of insane Italian highway driving. I was happy to be in the back seat. But it seems like there is some sort of agreement between all the drivers, and accidents are somehow avoided.

We picked up Salvatore, Vincenzo's boyfriend, and went immediately for PIZZA. The waiter smelled like ass but everyone only commented on his courtesy, so I kept quiet. The pizza was good, really good - and then we went for donut-hole-sized bombs filled with chocolate. AWESOME.

Salvatore lives with his sister and parents a little bit outside of Naples - on one of the hills - it was huge and immaculate and had three bedrooms and two bathrooms - ONE WITH A TUB! I can't remember the last time I saw one; it was like an archeological treasure.

Saturday we got up to the sight of Rosita, Salvatore's sister, setting up in the kitchen with a table full of profiteroles, filling them with cream, and then dipping them in chocolate sauce and building a mountain on a dessert tray. I almost passed out from joy when I saw it. Of course thought of you and your birthday dessert. She must have made a hundred; the whole table was covered in various stages of profiterolism.

We drove down into town again and had a really great, slow, long walk all along the waterfront - this was definitely NOT the Naples I saw last time! It was absolutely beautiful.

There is a little too much fascist architecture for my taste, but a lot of Naples is really pretty, in an Italy-has-forgotten-about-us way. We saw all these newlyweds getting their pictures taken by the water, and we cracked jokes and commented on the brides' attire. We also saw a groom feeling up his bride's ass during a picture session, and we totally called him on it! It was hilarious. I think we made our way into every wedding video.

We asked this lady and her friend to take our picture in Viola's favorite piazza, and the lady spent ten minutes positioning us just right. Her friend was making fun of her and I am sure the picture will be bizarre.

Naples is all lit up for Christmas already, and we walked for what seemed like miles through all these narrow streets packed with people and Christmas markets, and we went into several churches thanks to Vincenzo, who continues to amaze me with his quiet curiosity. I am so glad you met him - he is someone you either get or you don't - and it means so much to me that you understand how special he really is.

Miss Expatria

In Santa Chiara we saw a wedding - it was a huge church, so we were really far from the actual wedding, and there were a lot of people roaming around (all Italian tourists or Neopolitan; I did not see or hear one American or even non-Italian speaker at all). We took a pew and watched the whole end of the ceremony, and the procession out.

We got home and Viola and I took naps while they went and got Marco from the train station, and then we all had dinner that Rosita cooked - and Salvatore took credit for it! He was like, I salted the water just right - in the meantime Rosita had spent all day in the kitchen. Their friend Chiara came over for dinner, too - we had met her once in Rome - she is apparently obsessing over some kind of breakup so she and Viola got along famously.

And of course we attacked the mountain of profiteroles. Marco and I spoke your name in reverent tones.

As beautiful and warm as Saturday was, that's how ridiculously dark, cold and windy Sunday was. We got up and went to the market, which seemed to be in the middle of a field near a highway God only knows where. There were no tourists at all - I think I was the only non-Italian there, seriously - and there was a lot of stolen stuff.

I did not find any pants for you, and I did not find any shoes for me. I bought a really great watch for 3 euro, and a candlestick and two tiny teacup plates for my table in my room (which I have already filled with matchbooks and earrings). Marco found a pair of cords, and Viola bought a purse and slippers.

Miss Expatria

We went back to the house and had pranzo, and Marco and I finished the profiteroles. We bullshitted around the house for a while, and then went to dinner at a pizza place near Salvatore's house, not in the centro. We were escorted upstairs where the only other table was screaming 9-year-old girls at a birthday dinner. The waitress was just pissed off in general and plainly did not want to deal with us - she never even gave us menus, just expected us to know what we wanted - and opened the terrace door for the kitchen to cool down, which left us freezing. Vincenzo found us a table downstairs and things got better after that. The pizza was awesome, of course.

We were on a lot of the same streets from Saturday, but late at night, empty and pitch black, with a lot of trash and ownerless dogs roaming around, it was not quite the same shabby-chic it seemed to be - Naples is definitely one of those places where you want to find a fantastic hotel on the water and never leave it.

Monday we stopped at Chiara's bar to pick up pastries, and then took the drive back to Rome. Along the way we stopped at a cliff-side turn-off and ate the pastries and looked at the most stunning views of the sea and little islands on the horizon, and of course we were cracking jokes and being silly.

I really wish you could have been there, even though we would have had to tie one of us to the roof of the car to fit in Vince's tiny Punto.

Chapter Fourteen

2003-12-17

Marco and I went over Vincenzo's last night after work. His mom came up from Basilicata for the week and cooked for us, all kinds of stuff she made/grew and canned/brought from Basilicata.

- A wonderful, greasy, tomatoey, oniony type of bread soup (not brothy, SO GOOD).
- The best spicy sausages I have ever had, and that is saying something.
- Fresh cheese.
- Her marinated olives, eggplant, mushrooms, peppers.
- Her famous wine.
- Her bread.

She is this cliche of a tiny little old Italian widow who wears simple black or dark grey dresses, but she also wears these kick-ass, black leather, high-heel, knee-length boots. And she has the most mischievous smile.

She comes and spends a week or two with Vincenzo fevery once in a while. She cleans his house from top to bottom, cooks all his meals, and brings him a metric ton of food. I think if she ever went on an actual vacation, she wouldn't know what to do with herself.

2003-12-21

I went out on a date with a count! He is grown-up and suave and handsome! He lives in Switzerland and Italy! He took me for Indian food for my birthday! And we took taxis!

He kept apologizing for not getting me a present, and he wanted to take me shopping so I could pick something out, anything I wanted, and he would get it for me. While this was a tantalizing temptation, I told him it would mean more if he waited until he knew me better, and surprise me with something he picked out himself.

Wasn't that so demure of me? He'd better be happy Chanel didn't have any shoes I liked.

2004-01-01

My fabulous cousin Louis came over for the holidays again - I love him, and I love that he hops on a plane and comes to see me like it's no big deal. He just calls me and tells me when he's coming, and sure enough, on that day, my doorbell rings and it's like we had just seen each other 10 minutes ago.

On 12/31 we awoke at the crack of noon and I made the Duncan Hines cake that the gay mafia loves so much. We ran to Termini and got two bottles of Veuve - one for me, which I proceeded to drink directly out of the bottle to further insure that no one would take it, and the other for everyone else for midnight. Then we came back and Louis cut my hair - chopped it off! I absolutely love it. I think it took a while for the guys to get used to it, but after a half hour, Giovanni definitively proclaimed that it was beautiful. So I guess the verdict is in.

We had 10 people last night for New Year's. Much, much wine and champagne. Louis made our grandmother's chicken, which everyone loved, and Gianluca made a quiche, and Marco made tiny pizzas and puff pastries with asparagus and Gorgonzola stuffed inside and a tart with radicchio, speck and cheese. Viola also had this nasty, horrible fish thing - they never could explain it to me correctly. It looked like smoked sausage, and they cut it in slices, but it had the consistency of jellied fruit and tasted like salty ass. I had to spit it out and then eat like 60 crackers to get the taste out of my mouth.

At midnight here, everyone lights off fireworks. Off the tallest building in our piazza someone put on quite a show - huge, July 4th style. We all jammed onto our balcony and toasted and kissed and yelled AUGURI! at people walking by. Fireworks are one of my favorite things in the world and to have them be so close and BOOM loud and you could hear them going off all over the city, I don't think I will ever spend New Year's anywhere else.

Everyone went back inside and Marco and I spent a cigarette alone on the balcony. I told him 2003 was the best year of my life, one for the books. He said he was so happy to have been a part of it, and I had to turn away so as not to cry. What, I fear, would my life be like without this absolute angel of a man in it? What have I done in my life to deserve a friend like him?

We were talking about how much we love this life and our apartment, and he was joking about how we would be 60 years old together in this apartment, and oh how my heart ached for that to be true. One day this will all come to an end and to have to look at that man and say goodbye... I think I won't be able to do it. I think I will have to leave in the middle of the night.

We had lentils and cotechino when we came back in from the balcony, for tradition. Cotechino is like Spam wrapped in a thick layer of fat and boiled in a bag. Yeah, I know. The lentils were awesome though.

This afternoon I got up to find Marco the only one awake - his father had a stroke last night and his brother called early this morning to give him the news. He is sitting across from me now, staring down at the floor, smoking a cigarette - he just heard from his brother again, they had to resuscitate his dad just now. They don't want Marco to go to the hospital because they fear it will make his dad too emotional and they don't want him to have any kind of trauma. So he is kind of sitting around, staring, smoking.

To have this special, special friend in my life, whom I love so much and who I would do anything for, and to not be able to say or do the perfect thing at this moment to make everything all better - what a cruel joke. What a shitty New Year's Day.

Miss Expatria

2004-01-05

Louis and I rented a car and drove through the Appenine Mountains and it was just breathtaking, snowy caps and tiny mountainside villages and long tunnels and vertigo cliffs. We arrived in Pescara and drove along the coast for a while. At one point we got out of the car and walked across the beach to the edge of an angry, stormy Adriatic. I love winter beaches; it reminds me of where I grew up. I need to visit the sea more often.

We ambled our way blindly up to Citta S. Angelo, where our great-grandfather was born. It sits precariously on the top of a hill, and down every tiny street you can see sweeping views of the Adriatic on one side or the mountains on the other. When we entered the city, from the Adriatic side like one should, two dogs followed us and escorted us through the city walls.

It was after lunch and everyone seemed to be taking a nap, so it was like a ghost town that existed just for us to discover. It was just like I had dreamed, so many times, of going there, with Louis at my side. We snuck down the alleys and broke into courtyards and looked on doorbells for our family name, like it was our own personal playground. We went into an 8th-century church and saw St. Felicita's burial place. We ambled our way around and got as lost as one can in a tiny city perched on a hill.

On the way back through town the shops were all reopening, and Louis and I went into a jewelry store where he bought a beautiful white gold band. As Louis was looking around I told the owner that our great-grandfather was born there; when I told him our surname he recognized it immediately and said there were still some of us left there, and many years ago there had been a ton of us. As we were leaving, he gave Louis a calendar that features old pictures of the city. It's people like that who absolutely kill me in this country.

No matter where Italians wind up living, they always say they are from the town they were born in - it's called campanilismo, or "of the church bell tower." That man, the way he treated us, makes me believe in it. I could see him see us differently - like we belonged there. There I was, speaking my great-grandfather's language in his hometown with someone who knows his family.

We made record time back to Rome, gazing in wonder at moonlit snowcaps along the way, and had a fiasco trying to refill the gas tank - to sum it up, it involved a helpful stranger, us trying to sell gas to at least three motorinos, and return trips tomorrow to two gas stations for refunds.

Grandpop Giovanni: We love you and thought of you so much today; Louis said he could picture you running around those streets as a kid. I know you were watching us discover the one place in this world that runs through our veins like so much sweet red wine.

Miss Expatria

2004-01-06

This morning we awoke to find socks tied to our bedroom doorknobs with ribbon and filled with candy for the Epiphany, courtesy of Viola.

Pavlov Memento called me.

I am not angry or swooning over it; he's like an old friend from a past life. He is New York. He is everything to me, and nothing to me.

I have been promised a weekend in Venice, possibly for Carnivale, by The Count. Last night he texted me, *Are you sure you still want to be involved with me because I am a workaholic Virgo.*

I called him and said, "Listen to me. I am not going to freak out on you."

He breaks in with, "Yes, but I have had problems with this before with other women because when I work, I work too much."

I go, "LISTEN TO WHAT I AM TELLING YOU. I will not freak out on you. It is not my style. I have my own life here and I am a big girl. I know that when you have time for me we will be together and have a lot of fun. But I know the way you are with your work, and it is fine with me. IT IS FINE WITH ME. OK? Have you heard me?"

And he just completely melted and goes, "You are so unique and amazing, thank you so much, I have heard you, and I want you to know that when we are together, I forget everything else and I concentrate totally on you, you know that right?"

"Yes. That is why I am so patient."

"Well I am thinking of you and I miss you like crazy."

"Goodnight."

"Buona notte bella."

Doesn't that sound like a movie? That was our actual conversation!

I can hear Marco's beautiful voice in the other room, talking about his poor father.

Chapter Fifteen

London, January 15.

Because I am madcap and jetsetting, I decided to come and meet MK in London, where she is staying with our friends Heather and Matt. It's Friday morning; everyone else is still asleep.

Their apartment is like a little nest of love and warmth, and from their living room perch on the top floor I can look out onto a cinematically perfect London morning, all grey skies and brick and slate and chimney pipes, and across the street there is a Paddington Bear sitting in a window.

It really does exist. London!

I always thought I was being a ridiculous brat by wanting to take a cab from the airport to my destination when visiting a town for the first time, but I realized it really is the only way to do it when I was forced underground for untold amounts of time, navigating my way around peak fares and needing your ticket at the end and Circle Line and two Paddington stops and then up on the street, LOOK RIGHT and LOOK LEFT and wanting to look at everything else but for the Burger King that would tell me I was walking in the right direction from the train stop.

On their corner is St. Mary's Hospital, a huge old confection of a building where penicillin was invented, and all I can think about when I see it is the scene at the end of *The Little Princess* when she finds her dad. And all those films where there are the courageous, wounded British soldiers in iron beds having their foreheads wiped clean by an improbable-looking nurse.

"Wehh you veddy brave Tawmy? Tawmy, can you heahh me daahling?"

After finally being able to understand a foreign language, how very disconcerting it is not to understand people who are clearly speaking in my native tongue, directly to me, in context.

We went for Indian food last night, where I proceeded to have the best butter chicken known to mankind. Cinnamony, buttery, cardamomy, it really was delicious; and when I told the ancient waiter, he called ME delicious. How fabulous are waiters who call people delicious?

It was an outstanding meal, but Matt told me that on Saturday we are going to the "good" place. I can only IMAGINE what it is going to be like, if this was their "ok" local spot.

When British guys are hot, they are WHITE HOT; but when they are ugly, they really are something to behold.

Also, lace curtains in the windows! Everywhere! Cute.

Poor Matt is off the whole weekend, and apparently is sticking it out here with us. He was clearly overwhelmed, while trying ever so quietly to watch a program about World War II, by mine and MK's non-stop chatter and non-sequitoring from one subject to the next. He was shocked when he would find we were talking to him - mostly to ask him to open another bottle of wine, or when Heather was coming home from work, or how he liked the cheese I brought.

He is a good, Britishly tolerant man and definitely needs to be awarded some sort of medal if he can survive til Monday with the three of us. We have nicknamed him Bosley since the three of us are so clearly kick-ass-fabulous, and we are also a blonde, a brunette and a redhead.

London is the result of someone taking New York and pushing it through some sort of time-space-language sieve. You know how when you're little you think you can dig to China from your hole on the beach, or that Australians walk on their heads because they are on the bottom of the world? That is London to me. It is not even real.

London, January 16

Saturday morning. We all just got up and it is a gloriously sunny day! Matt is about to make bacon sarnies and MK is making scones and it is so strange that we are grown ups and are allowed to do things like spend a weekend together in London.

Miss Expatria

Yesterday we rode on a double decker bus and took pictures. We saw the only store in London that sells barrister's wigs and cloaks. We looked for 84 Charing Cross Road, but it's a Pizza Express now.

Heather used the word "plinth" in conversation.

I also heard the following Best English Accented Quote Ever: "Ihht's naught chaisy, yow've nivah fooking beeean theyuhh!"*

"It's not cheesy, you've never fucking been there!"

Last night we met up with MK's friend Alison at the Lonsdale. We had about a hundred dishes of tiny, exquisite foods, and bellinis made with red grapes and honey. Then we went to the Cow and drank untold amounts of wine, all of us on tiny low pub stools in a packed pub. After last call we went to Beach Party Babylon, a labyrinthine place that served us more amazing bellinis.

Gotta go, Matt just brought me my VERY FIRST BACON SANDWICH with something called brown sauce.

Stansted Airport, Monday 19 January.

Of course I petered out on faithfully updating my journal after the first full day.

First things first: The bacon sarnie was wonderful.

Miss Expatria

Saw Big Ben; it was much shorter and squatter than I thought it would be.

Then to Parliament and Buckingham Palace. The Palace looked like a government building in DC to me; I must say I was completely unimpressed. Had a Snapple Lemonade nearby that cost 3 pounds sterling.

Walked through St. James Park, lovely; many strange birds; saw a COOT, which is a very funny bird, many geese and several black swans with red beaks. St. James Park is also home to what can only be described as the world's fattest pigeons.

We also saw the changing of the horse guard somewhere, which was really neat as there was no one there to block us off; we all kind of milled around as they did sillywalks and shouted instructions and stared straight ahead. It was like peeking in on something we were not supposed to see.

Saturday night we went to a pub where I saw WEST END GIRLS in their finest. They are exact replicas of their chi-chi-bar-going counterparts in New York and completely uninteresting. Now I need to find EAST END BOYS.

Sunday was AFTERNOON TEA at Claridge's. We had champagne tea and plates of tiny delicate sandwiches and the best scones on earth and another plate filled with tiny desserts. It was all very refined and so lovely. I could do that every day, just have that be my meal of the day.

I also went to M&S and bought two pairs of jeans, lacy boy-cut underwear and a pajama pants set.

Miss Expatria

All in all it was a really nice trip, if hellaciously expensive.

London. I did not love it; it is too much like New York. It did not fascinate me. I felt like I knew it already. But I had a good time with my girls, laughing and being led to fabulous places and just being in London to be there.

2004-01-21

Today I had to wait at home for an architect to come over and measure our living room. I think it had something to do with having our living room be in regulation, which I would say is impossible since I don't believe there is a right angle to be had in the whole place. The living room was built later than the rest of the place; it kind of sticks out in a courtyard made by four adjoining buildings. It would be akin to a sunroom, if whomever built it had had the foresight to put larger windows in it.

So, this architect: She was extremely well dressed and had 19 different kinds of measuring tape that came out of a gorgeous leather Mary Poppins-looking bag. I had to help her measure stuff in between her taking cell phone calls and smoking cigarettes and talking to me constantly about everything she was doing. She was quite fabulous.

2004-01-27

Salvatore showed up suddenly yesterday, in full Gay Italian Melodrama, unable to eat, sleep or work because Vincenzo wanted to break up with him. It was tense in Romalife yesterday, what with Salvatore bursting randomly into tears and all of us ignoring him. Then today, we picked them up in Marco's car and they were fine. I need a scorecard to keep track here.

Anyway, we drove over to Pyramide and had late night pastry, which as usual is God's Gift to Food, and then we parked and took a long walk through Campo di Fiori, Piazza Navona, and all around those tiny vicoli in between.

Just walking so slow, strolling really, and looking into people's apartments and bullshitting and laughing and having one of those evenings where I have to fall back a little for a minute because my eyes suddenly fill with tears of absolute, unbridled happiness.

I am going to be out of a job before the end of the year, because of this shitting merger of our clients' company with another. MK told me all about it when we were in London - I used to work with her at the agency, but now I kind of work for her, I guess - the client stole her away from us!

Anyway, she explained how the merger meant that our client would moving all of the work we do, in-house. It won't be just me who'll be out of a job; but I don't see how I could conceivably look for new work from all the way over here.

This hits me particularly hard on nights like last night; now I know for sure that this won't go on forever, and someone is standing so close to my precious bubbleworld with the longest pin, cackling, ready and oh so willing to take this perfect life away from me. It makes me lose my breath, and I want to hold on to the nearest crumbling wall or thousand-year-old column and never let go.

2004-02-05

I was just outside and this mom and her little boy, holding a paper bag, came around the corner. He sees me, walks directly over to me, and says (in Italian), "Want to see what I have in the bag?"

"OK, sure."

He opens the bag and we both peer inside. He tells me all about the action figures he has in there.

"They are so nice!"

"I know!" He continued talking about them over his shoulder as he ran to catch up to his mom.

I am never, ever leaving.

Chapter Sixteen

2004-02-06

Friday night Vincenzo and I took the train south to Caserta. It was packed so we sat in the baggage compartment, which was quite nice actually, with three strangers. At one point we opened some wine and all five of us had a toast! Also, Vincenzo bought cheese and salami and bread and made sandwiches for all of us.

Salvatore, who apparently is back in Vnicenzo's good graces, and his cousin Mariella met us at the train station. We drove up the mountain to Salvatore's little house there. It has the most unbelievable views of other peaks in front of it and then a whole valley and then another mountain range. The ride up the mountain was scary, with hairpin turns like the kind you see in car commercials.

When we got to the tiny, crumbling house, we lit a fire and Vincenzo made pasta with his mom's sauce, which ALWAYS ROCKS. Then we stayed up and chatted all night. Mariella and I slept downstairs, next to the fire.

Miss Expatria

2004-02-07

Saturday we bummed around, ate risotto with artichokes, and we grilled artichokes on the fire as well. Then Salvatore's cousin Enzo came with Anna, his girlfriend of a kabillion years. He was SO HOT, I could barely look at him.

They all spoke in strong Naples dialect, so I spent most of the night feeling like an idiot. But Vincenzo told me he doesn't understand half of what they say either, so I felt a little better.

I was keeping Vincenzo company while he was cooking, and he cut me a piece of pecorino romano cheese, which is my favorite. I took a bite, sighed, and said, "Adoro pecorina." Vincenzo snapped his head around to look at me, and started howling laughing. He runs in and tells the rest of them what I said, and then they too were crying with laughter.

It turns out that while I wanted to say I love Roman goat's milk cheese, I actually was standing there, eating a piece of cheese, and ruminating about how much I love to have sex doggie-style.

The vowels. The vowels will surely be the death of me.

Miss Expatria

2004-02-08

Sunday we all got up late-ish and had an enormous pranzo - more risotto with artichokes, pasta with lemon sauce, grilled sausages, salad, and a frittata with mortadella. And more wine than most third world countries could drink in 10 years, all courtesy of Vincenzo's mom.

Hot Enzo told me he wanted to date me so he could learn English, and followed me around yelling my name and listing the words he knew in English; I was simultaneously swooning and avoiding him because Anna was not pleased.

We cleaned up the house and bummed around some more, then drove even further up the mountain to this beautiful, beautiful lake. It was iced over and snowy and so lovely; Mariella and I stayed by the car and smoked and chatted while the rest of them went down to the lake's edge and threw snow at each other.

We drove back down the mountain in this huge awful super scary dense fog. I thought we were going to die about 700 times. I will never, ever do that again. I swear I would have stayed in a hotel on the lake if I had known. I wound up hiding and whimpering behind Mariella, who was screaming, as the guys gasped at every turn the car made. It was horrible.

We finally, finally, got below the fog line and then it was just plain hair-raising. When we got out of the car at the train station I wanted to kiss the ground, Pope-style.

Miss Expatria

2004-02-12

Last night Giovanni treated us all to Indian, because he was
craving Tandoori chicken and wanted company. It was
awesome. The guy knows us at the restuarant, because
there are always at least three of us, and we always come
rushing in the door in a junkie frenzy, wild-eyed and
drooling and demanding plates of naan. Then we eat like
men condemned and go into a post-Indian-food coma while
Giovanni orders the inevitable second plate of Tandoori
chicken, and we smoke and watch him tear apart the
chicken and get the spices all over his face. I am sure we
are a sight to behold.

We went over Vincenzo's after, and watched old *San Remo*
tapes and made fun of Ana Oxa. I had a dessert that
featured pig's blood and chocolate as its two main
ingredients, which freaked me out, BECAUSE IT WAS
GOOD.

As we were walking to his car, along his beautiful,
decrepit, aquaduct-lined street, laughing and changing
words to songs and tired and full, we passed a tiny, lit niche
with a statue of the Madonna and candles and flowers, and
I thought to myself, how will this end? How can I spend
my remaining time here not constantly on the verge of
tears? How can these men be more important to me, closer
to me, than almost anyone else in my life?

Chapter Seventeen

2004-02-13

Left work at 3:45 and took the train up to Milan. Was in a compartment with five surprisingly normal and quiet people. Spent the last hour alone, save an Indian guy who tried to accost me; but a loud NON MI TOCCARE and a backhand across the face while wearing my gigantic ring sent him scurrying.

The Count drove down from Switzerland to pick me up because he is a classy, mature guy. It's my first drive across an international border while on a date!

2004-02-14

We bummed around Lugano for a while. It's beautiful but too clean for my taste, too efficiently run, too... Swiss. We ate at a kind of Swiss diner and I had rosti, which is like a hashbrown pancake, with an egg.

We went home and I ran a bath with excellent Oceanus bath bubbles from the Body Shop - you never know how much you miss a bath until you're forced to shower in prefab stalls that you can't even turn around in, they're so small. I get really tired of not being able to shave my legs while in the shower.

He sat in the bathroom with me while I soaked in a mountain of bubbles, feeding me Valpolicella wine and white Swiss chocolate dipped in Skippy peanut butter, and lighting our cigarettes, and we talked about absolutely everything and anything for about two hours. It wasn't sexual at all - but it was very, very decadent. He treats me like such a princess! I think he has no idea what to do with me.

2004-02-15

The Count did not believe me when I told him that I do not function when awakened at 7:30AM by an alarm clock. We drove cross the Swiss-Italian border blasting *Frank Sinatra at the Sands with Count Basie*; eventually I became a functioning human being, and then we arrived in Venice. After a fine pizza lunch outside in the sun, I expertly led him to Piazza San Marco, with the map of Venice that was burned into my soul during my first visit, in January of last year with my cousin Louis.

It was when Louis had come to keep me company during my first Christmas out of th States. I was still living in Lavinio, and we were bored out of our skulls in a town where not only were the majority of businesses closed for the winter; those remaining were closed for the holidays.

We went into Rome, bought cheap tickets to Venice, and went for a couple days. I remember getting off the traghetto, or public transport boat, and coming into Piazza

San Marco. You make that left and the whole piazza unfolds before you. You're freaking out but then you look to your right and HOLY CRAP it's the basilica OH MY GOD. It was that moment when I realized that Venice might be the coolest place on earth, and I proceeded to memorize it so as to kep it with me at all times.

And now here I was, a little over a year later, with a count at Carnivale! A mix of Phladelphia's Mummer's Parade and *Eyes Wide Shut*. Fabulous. FABULOUS!

We walked around and purposely got lost a bit, and he kissed me on tiny empty streets. We made our way back to Piazza San Marco and watched the doings of so, so many people. He listens better than I thought he does, because although I had only mentioned Harry's Bar and Hemingway and bellinis once when he picked me up in Milan, I suddenly found myself at a table in said bar with said drink placed in front of me, The Count laughing at my bliss.

Then we returned to the car and drove back to Switzerland, listening to the radio, talking again about everything and everything. We were starving when we got back to Lugano, but it was late on a Sunday night and nothing was open. I bet not many people can say this: I ate dinner with a count at a Burger King in Switzerland.

Miss Expatria

2004-02-16

There is little greater feeling than that of being on the Eurostar, pulling into Rome, and having it feel like home. Near tears again from the sheer happiness of living here, of having this city be the place to which I return from all these amazing experiences. Can I ever love anyone again, when this place so clearly has seduced me, addicting me to it?

Chapter Eighteen

2004-02-18

The boss of my bosses just called me. She said:

1. She has a close friend at our client who says the merger has a more aggressive timeframe than originally anticipated.

2. She wanted to tell me, since the merger has the ability to mess with my life more than everyone else's.

3. She is jealous of my situation and wants me to be able to continue living here, so she is going to see if she can give me anther piece of client business so I can keep living here INDEFINITELY.

This is the first time I have ever spoken to the woman. I am now in love with her and want to have 10,000 of her babies.

Miss Expatria

2004-02-20

Last night, radiatore with sausage and zucchini. And cheese, and mandarines, and a spoonful of Nutella.

There was some kind of freaky storm last night and now all of Rome is covered in pinkish orange sand that was swept up from the Sahara desert and dumped all over the region. I can go outside right now and touch African sand.

2004-03-03

Last night was Italy's 54th, and my second, *San Remo* music festival. It sucked just as much as the 53rd, which was my first, but the thing that made it better was I understood more and we all made bitchy, hilarious comments and I laughed so hard I lost my breath. Vincenzo's mom's sauce made another appearance, as did roast beef that Marco brought back from Bologna with his mom's blessing.

I walked to work in the bitter cold because the bus driver - intentionally, I thought - rammed into the mirror of a double-parked Mercedes SUV and a huge screaming match ensued. While Italian arguments are an endless source of amusement for me, I really had to get to work.

Miss Expatria

2004-03-10

I think I met someone. I mean, I did meet someone - but I think he could be SOMEONE. Because, frankly, there is no way that meeting this guy was not meant to be in some way.

Viola and I found a cheapo flight to Montpellier, France, where her cousin and his wife live. It's in the south, kind of on the coast, I think? Anyway, we decided to be madcap and go for it.

Montpellier is gorgeous. Luca, Viola's cousin, picked us up at the train station, and we walked up a beautiful street lined with palm trees - hello, South of France! - which opened into an enormous piazza. Place de la Comedie, it's called. The borders of the piazza are lined with cafes, all with outdoor seating, and an over-the-top confection of an opera house, and it's all so very French and ooh la la.

We got settled at the house and his wife, Daniela, came home from work. We had the most amazing dinner, all cold foods - sausages, cheeses, bread, olives, fish, a hundred other things - it was so rustic and delicious. They kept apologizing, but it was amazing!

Viola kept whining about wanting to go out on the town - apparently, Montpellier is over 50 percent students, and she wanted to know where all the American students hang out. Luca gave us directions down tiny little winding streets to an Irish pub. I went along with her idea; I figured it would be good to speak English, and maybe Viola could practice her flirting, since frankly, she sucks at it.

Miss Expatria

The place was enormous and solid, with walls made of stone; we got seats at the bar and I ordered our drinks from the Irish-est bartender this side of Cork.

Viola was so chatty and excited, and we made plans for the rest of the weekend based on some recommendations from Luca and Daniela. After I ordered the next round, this guy came up to me and said, "Excuse me, I just have to know - are you English or Italian?"

I said I was neither: American. He says he's American (even though he kind of has a Eurofag accent); he's from New Jersey.

I almost fell off my stool. Talk of Parkway exits commenced. At one point I had to stop and translate for Viola, who was sitting there quietly fuming that no one had come up to her.

He said he approached me because he had heard me speaking in Italian and then ordering my drinks in perfect English. I told him I was fluent in Italian, because I live in Rome. (It felt so weird to say that to someone from New Jersey, for some reason; I can't remember the last time I told someone I live in Rome. *I live in Rome!*)

He asks me what I do for a living, and I start in on the kind of work I do, halfway apologizing because I know no one ever understands. He stops me and says, no, I know exactly what you mean, I do the same thing!

Miss Expatria

TWO PEOPLE FROM NEW JERSEY WHO WORK FREELANCE IN EUROPE ARE CHATTING IN AN IRISH PUB IN THE SOUTH OF FRANCE. It sounds like the beginning of a joke!

He started explaining how he works, which kind of sounded like eBay but for freelance writing jobs. If he wins a project, he and sometimes his designer work on the project, submit it online, and get paid online directly into their bank accounts.

I must have asked him about a million questions. At some point he tells me, just come to the Internet place where I work (!!) and I'll show you, it's easier to see it in action.

He gave me directions and we exchanged names, and he left me to recount all of this craziness to Viola. I could not get over what had just happened. She was non-plussed, but I was freaking out.

The rest of the weekend was so relaxing and French. Luca and Daniela took us out for a drive through miles of countryside and tiny crumbling villages, and we had lunch in this tinsy tinsy piazza in a tinsy tinsy bistro. We took them out to dinner at a place of their choice back in Montpellier, which was so delicious I almost died - and the prix fixe menu was a joke, cost-wise.

It was weird to speak Italian and then French, with no English at all to be had. I felt quite the linguist.

I went to the Internet place and there was the guy from the Irish pub, hunched over a keyboard. I asked him why he didn't have his own computer, and he said his ex-wife took it as well as most everything else he owned when she left. YIKES. Didn't push for that story.

He showed me the site and how it works, and I think I might be able to do it as well - I'm going to set up my own account when I go back to Rome, and see what kind of administrative jobs are on there.

But mostly, I was kind of into HIM. Cal, his name is. He's cute; but more than how he looked, he was just so BRILLIANT and SMART - he talks fast, like he has more ideas than he can fit in his head and they spill out. And all those ideas seem to make him not have enough room to be aware of the world around him. He's kind of like an absent-minded professor.

Anyway, that was the weekend. Since then, we've been talking online during the workday, and he is really cool, really on it. He is the opposite of Pavlov Memento in every way possible. And I really, really like talking to him.

2004-03-12

So yesterday, MK calls me and tells me that the merger has been moved up a month, to June 1, and that things are moving really, really quickly; more quickly than that big boss said when she called me. So nothing will happen before then, but after that, no one knows.

I think I have the summer here. Maybe I can do this freelance stuff, but for admin-type work, on that site that Cal uses?

Miss Expatria

2004-03-13

Here is an interesting email exchange with a friend of mine,
Francesco, from Milan:

*Francesco: I can't explain exactly the BLUE: It is a mood,
a way of feeling passion, a well-balanced passion. A love
for life, deep, passionate but in someway cold, or cool...*

*Me: ...an objective view of the presence of passion, while
one is feeling it, and you are able to still be in the moment.
It is when I have been sitting around a table with my best
friends for hours, and there are plates still on the table, and
we pour the last of the last of the wine, and someone says
something that cracks us all up, and I have to sometimes
turn away because I get choked up at the perfection of
living the exact life I want to be living a the exact moment I
am living it.*

*It is having the first coffee of the day at 4pm after having
spent all day in bed, and reading the paper, and not having
to speak, and there is no need to constantly proclaim that
the passion is there, because it is always there, just below
the surface of life's everyday activities. Well, at least that
would be MY definition of what you are saying. Sorry if I
totally missed the point.*

*Francesco: You didn't miss the point, you understood even
better than me what I was trying to say. I couldn't give a
better definition. What you say is deeply thoughtful,
charming, delicate and still powerful. "Feel passion, and
not having to speak" - this is exactly what I think when I*

say "passion of blue." The things you say and the style you use are fascinating.

Me: Your kind words made my otherwise crap day, thank you. I just know how I want to live my life and I never settle for anything less than that. I don't see the point in living otherwise. "Living life to the fullest" is a horrible cliche and is so often mistaken to mean quests for power and dominance in any and all categories of life; but in the end, the people who say they have lived life to the fullest look back and see that in their race to conquer they have missed the small quiet moments that make up a life passionately lived. I propose we strike this misused cliche from the language and replace it with "Find the passion of blue." I like it better.

Tell me, how do you want to live your life?

2004-03-15

Woke up slowly and lazily. Came out of my room to find:

1) A bottle of Veuve left at my door by Giovanni
2) Giovanni, in rare form, doing his diva thing
3) Marco cleaning the house and laughing at Gio, and shaking out the rugs over the balcony
4) All the windows and shutters open, and a fine March breeze racing through the hallways and rooms
5) A pack of cigs that Marco had bought for me, since I still am waiting for my new debit card and have no money

6) All my stuff from the washing machine already on the stendino, courtesy of Marco

Then I walked into the kitchen, where I found:

1) A tray of pastries Gio brought over
2) Marco cooking sausages and eggs and toasting bread
3) An open bottle of red wine with a glass waiting for me

2004-03-18

I've been talking to Cal online every day as we both do our work, and it's awesome. He is awesome.

We live completely different lives; he loves being the outsider, and has a whole little English-speaking world he lives in in Montpellier, and his life is very small in how he lives it; he loves his routine. I dove headfirst into being Roman, and although my days do have a rhythm, almost anything can happen at any time.

Anyway, he invited me to come and work with him and Jonty, his designer, for a few days, to get a feel for how it all works. And I accepted! I'm flying to Paris, and taking the TGV train down to Montpellier, and staying with Jonty and his wife in their kickass apartment!

The gay mafia is all giddy and excited for me, although I tried to play it down. As I was on my way to bed, Gio called out to me, in English:

Miss Expatria

"THE GAY MAFIA WILL ALWAYS PROTECT YOU DARLING!"

I know you will.

2004-03-23

On the way to work today, I was walking down via Urbana and saw a workman hook up an old lady's shopping bags to his pulley hanging off the building so that she could walk up to her no-doubt-fabulous, top-floor apartment unencumbered.

The Roman accent is no doubt my very favorite accent ever. You hear a bunch of guys standing around and one of them is ostensibly complaining about some injustice, but you can see he is relishing the telling of the story, with the hands flying, and the fabulous accent, and even though he is clearly working himself into a lather, he is half laughing and his friends are all kind of laughing along with him.

I can't describe it; it's something you have to hear to really love. It's not nasal, like in the north; not too glutteral, like in the South. Like Rome itself, it is a perfect mix of both, and it flows better than other accents; I am able to speak more quickly if I use a Roman accent than if I try to speak schoolbook Italian. I guess I am also talking about the dialect as well, because the Roman dialect is so much fun and juicy and something I have had a lot of fun adopting.

Of course, my friends all say I speak with an American accent, which I am sure is true; but in my mind, I sound like such a Roman.

Chapter Nineteen

2004-03-29

Montpellier. On the train on the way down here from Paris on Saturday, it occurred to me that maybe Cal wasn't really serious about his invitation, and that I was hurtling along at 200mph towards a huge, huge mistake.

Then I got off the train and he was there, and I realized it was all worth it.

He's working five feet away from me right now, which is fun.

2004-03-31

Cal's life in Montpellier is like if Hunter S. Thompson wrote "A Year in Provence," and Salvador Dali provided the illustrations.

Miss Expatria

2004-04-01

Last night we went to Fitz but it was too early for Fizz so we went to an all-night epicerie and got bread and dried sausage and ham and ate with all the candles everywhere and told each other stories and made each other laugh really hard and then in the middle of one of my stories he blew out all the candles and found me in the dark and we didn't get to sleep until much later.

2004-04-02

Email from me to Vincenzo:

HOW ARE YOUR ENGLISH LESSONS DARLING

LOVE YOU

KISSES

Email from Vincenzo to me:

I like my english lessons, happy danger.

I love you

2004-04-05

I finally got home last night, and was greeted by Gio, Vince and Marco, jumping up and down and taking my bags and leading me into the living room where there was wine waiting for me and Marco was cooking me a huge bowl of pasta Bolognese and they were screaming about how it was obvious I hadn't eaten in days because I was so skinny. Then they grilled me about my week. God, I missed my boys.

Life is to be molded to one's will, one's desire; life is a plaything to sit back and watch unfold and laugh at what you have made happen, because they are always your dreams come to life in front of your eyes. Remember this.

2004-04-08

I realized that not having an end date here was the thing that was really bothering me. So I made one: October 1. I ideally need to stay here until then for tax purposes, give or take about two weeks. So I am going to do all I can to stay here until then, whatever it takes, then I'm going back to the States. If it so happens that, in my working it out to stay here until October, I can stay later, great. If I need to shave a couple weeks off October 1, then that's what I'll have to do. But October 1 is my goal.

2004-04-10

Am somehow functioning through a low-grade panic attack after having a dream about 9/11. I dreamt I touched a steel beam from the WTC that hung from a ceiling in a room near NYU, where I went to school. The enormity of it all hit me and I cried so hard in that dream, the soul-ripping kind of crying, but woke up not crying.

Forgot to take a shower, got dressed and came here. Forgot my cell phone, my student loan stuff, my cigs. Not really able to see anything very clearly. Am trying to remember to breathe. Am trying not to completely lose it.

Fuck you, New York. I'm coming back, fuck you.

2004-04-11

The sun has finally shown itself, and it was at the perfect angle on the house on the corner of via Baccina, making shadows from the hanging ivy that is creeping across the telephone wire, and the shutters against the ochre walls. Leaned against the wall and looked up and saw a cloud formation that looked just like Italy, complete with Sicily, and I also watched a woman maintaining her roof garden. It was blissfully quiet. It was a perfect five minutes.

2004-04-12

Giovanni was on a huge TV show here the other day, and I snuck into Viola's room to watch him. He is adopted and just found out 10 years ago, and he went on the show and told his story and asked that anyone with any information about his birth family to write to him. He was awesome.

He explained to me later that he needed to do that because there is a law here prohibiting adopted children from learning about their birth families, even for health reasons, because year ago there were several incindents involving grown children who had discovered they were adopted, found their birth parents and killed them. Holy crap.

The show he was on is called *Piazza Grande*, and the set is made to look like a typical piazza but in pastel colors and so, so cheesy. They have serious interviews like the one with Gio, and then they hop up and yell, contest time! And the host calls people at home to play a game for money and half of them are like, no thanks. Or they break into old musical numbers. It is hilarious.

2004-04-15

I just saw three middle-aged women freak out because a black cat crossed their path.

On Easter, I woke up to someone on the other side of the street playing "Overjoyed" by Stevie Wonder, which is a lovely way to wake up if you ask me. Marco was in the kitchen already working on pranzo. We had spinach and ricotta ravioli, and grilled sausages, and fried garlic on lettuce leaves, and hard-boiled eggs. And then we opened the enormous chocolate Easter egg that Gio gave us; it's a thing here instead of Easter baskets - a huge chocolate hollow egg, the size of a football, with a toy inside. We got a Spiderman racecar.

Played more Burraco, and now he has gone to charge his dad's car battery. After buying me cigs. BEST GAY HUSBAND EVER.

2004-04-23

I went to Montpellier again! Cal met me at the train station he gave me a copy of *American Tabloid* by James Ellroy, because it is his favorite book and he wanted me to read it.

Miss Expatria

Spent an hour in the bookstore, talking about books we love and hate and writers we love and hate. Spent an hour at the English language movie theater, talking about films we love and hate, and films we will see this weekend.

We went to the crazy fondue place for a goodbye dinner for Clive, who showed up late and left early, so it turned out to be a better time than expected. Clive is from Liverpool and has some kind of important job at the IBM headquarters here. Apparently, everyone from Liverpool is crazy.

Vic, who is also from Liverpool and also crazy, came to dinner and I love her to bits, she is just down to earth and totally cool. The dinner featured big pots of boiling cheese and chocolate and wine served in baby bottles.

I have no idea what I am doing here. But Jesus, is he brilliant. And we connect on a level I have never known.

Saturday. Read at an outdoor cafe in the sun for five hours, breaking silences only to discuss the books we were reading, having one comment turn into a huge discussion about the myth of King Arthur and religion and American political history, then falling back into silence to continue reading.

Went to Fitz and played backgammon outside with various expats. Went for Indian food.

Sunday. Went for B R U N C H, yes, brunch, my all-time favorite meal, at a restaurant owned by his friends, a lesbian couple named Lu and Mu. Mimosas. Eggs Benedict. Yes please!

Monday. Home. Vincenzo, Gio and Marco arrived home a half-hour after me. Hilarity, lasagna, and fresh roasted pork ensued.

2004-05-10

My upcoming travel plans:

- San Sebastian with MK, John, Heather and Matt for lots of sangria and a 3-Michelin-star dinner 5/14 - 17
- London for most yummiest Indian dinner 5/17
- Montpellier, once again 5/18 - 5/22
- Rich comes to Rome 5/23 - 26
- Venice Memorial Day weekend with Rich 5/29 - 31

All my charges went through for this plane ticket-buying extravaganza. So I'm booked!

The police are shutting Cal's entire apartment building down at 4PM due to numerous code violations. He is getting a one-bedroom from the same landlord for the same price as his studio. His life is like a Bukowski story.

2004-05-14

I am sitting on a bed in a hotel room with a terrace on the sixth floor, overlooking the Bay of Biscay in San Sebastian, Spain.

Tonight I am going to sleep to the sound of crashing waves, and then begin eating and drinking again with my friends, and giggling a lot.

I love being a grown-up.

2004-05-15

Tapas-hopping last night was one of the more fun experiences of my life. Heather, Matt, MK and I all put money in a kitty and John, MK's husband, held onto it and paid for everything. At the end of the night, we still had 20 euro left. We went back to La Concha, a bar on the beach, and sat outside and ate about 63 desserts, one of which had a HOT BROWNIE in the middle of a bowl of ice cream.

Tapas places - you just walk in, order your drink, and start grazing on all the yummy treats laid out on the bar. Then you settle up, sometimes by counting toothpicks, and move on to the next place.

Tapas are God's gift to mankind. It is the most perfect type of food ever invented. I only want food served to me tapas style from now on, with the exception of my beloved cacio e pepe, which must be served in an enormous, deep, white ceramic bowl.

Today we took a long slow walk all around and had lunch at some amazing tapas bar that was written up in the New York Times two weeks ago. We sat at a long table on benches and had several rounds of drinks and 35 pieces of tapas. I ate two pieces of foie gras tapas yumminess, which was hands-down the best thing I have EVER EATEN.

Miss Expatria

Tapas here are called pintxos I think, or some combination of those letters in the bizarre Spanish-but-not-Spanish language that looks like a cross between pig latin and Icelandic. It's such a relief to just leave all of the talking up to John and not have to think at all about language.

Just woke up from a delicious nap. I pulled the pillows to the foot of the bed so I could go to sleep while staring at the sea and the beach and have the breeze hit me. Snuggled under a great heavy blanket and slept off lunch. Have lovely healthy color on my face from walking in the sunshine yesterday and today.

Waves crashing and far off voices speaking another language, sleepy.

2004-05-16

Last night was chichi dinner at a place on a cliff overlooking the sun dipping into the Bay of Biscay. It was really good, and not ridiculously expensive (by New York standards, at least), though I find that since living in Rome, expensive meals that require the server to explain how to eat each complicated course are not as fulfilling as a retardedly simple dish that is exquisite and like 4 euro. I've changed.

Today we lounged around at breakfast, and they were hemming and hawing about where to go and what to do. They finally asked me and I said, I think we should drive to Biarritz, France and have lunch, because it is the most bitchily elegant thing I can think of. So we drove along the coast, had lunch in Biarritz, hung out, and came back. It was, in fact, the most bitchy and elegant thing ever. On the way back we blasted bad 80's music and sang "Jessie's Girl" really loudly and offkey across the border and the soldiers just shook their heads and waved us through.

2004-05-18

Monday, flew to London for dinner. Tuesday morning, hopped on a flight to Montpel. This is living.

2004-05-20

Montpel: I've become intrigued by the cheese aisles in French supermarkets. They are something to behold.

We read again in the piazza and drank citron presses. Ate really good croissants. Bought train ticket to Paris. Bought Metallica concert DVD for Cal. He invited me to come to Montpel and watch the elections with him in November.

This whole week of my travels - how strange it is to have absolute perfection be the norm. My life is bliss. There's no way it can get better than this.

Chapter Twenty

2004-05-25

Back in Rome. Rich is here on vacation. It's fun to talk to him in our own way; I am a different kind of friend with him than I am with anyone else. I met him through my best friend from college, Howie; even though I have known Rich for years, I still feel like he was my first grown-up friend. Maybe it's because he has a grown-up finance job; maybe it's just because we talk about things I remember grown-ups talking about when I was little.

We went to Ditirambo last night for dinner, his choice. We had to travel way the hell across town to get there. We go in and he doesn't like the table, so I talk to the host and we get it changed. I translated the entire menu for him and he picked a bottle of wine that was way more expensive than it should have been. We had to order different things so he could taste as much as possible.

After all this, I ask him how he liked the place, and he says, "It didn't change my world." I wanted to lean across the table and bitch-slap him.

But, despite all this, he is one of my favorite dinner companions in the whole wide world - he swoons like I do when tasting something great, and we never are at a loss for words. And I love to make him laugh, because it seems to take him by surprise.

2004-05-26

Rich is off in Florence for a few days. Vincenzo, Salvatore and I went to Domus Aurea for free today. It's Nero's subterranean palace. It was awesome, and a bit creepy, but SO NICE AND CHILLY. We agreed to remember that place when it gets hotter than hell this summer.

Went into La Voglia for a spicy salami sandwich with spicy cheese; it has been a while since I have gotten a sandwich from there. La voglia, as a phrase, means the desire or the yearning. I love that.

It smells so good in La Voglia. I could just stand in there for like an hour and breathe deeply. Its smell is second only to my beloved South Jersey WaWa's. And, La Voglia bizarrely sells Skippy peanut butter. So, you know, it's one of my top ten places in Rome.

Gio is back from Berlin (cue bad Italian music). I missed him so much! We got caught up last night over wine and cigs while Marco cooked. Salvatore and Vincenzo came over, and we all chowed down on radiatore with sausage and zucchini. Then I went to bed and slept 11 hours.

I was lolling in bed at 11AM this morning, thinking of all the annoying ways I am awakened each day. And then I realized that among this list, nowhere does an alarm clock appear, and so then all the annoying things immediately became precious and quite sentimental to me:

- trash truck
- honking horns due to blocking of street by trash truck
- the butcher department of the grocery store whose entrance is around the corner, hacking meat and sliding meat on the racks directly below my bedroom
- a bitchy, yippy dog who comes with some guy to the bar downstairs every day around 10:30, and stands outside and bitchily yips at everyone who passes by
- Viola's heels as she goes back and forth from her room to the bathroom 1,500 times before work
- the squeaky gate door to the building's courtyard across the street
- our buzzer ringing to let in the postman or the cleaning ladies because we are the first bell on the list
- Marco knocking on my door in an attempt to wake me up before he leaves
- whistle blows from soccer coach at the field up the street
- 5,000 "ciao"s as various people greet each other and then part ways on the street
- the lady across the street who talks to her friend on the phone every day while leaning out her window and smoking

Miss Expatria

2004-06-03

MK wrote to say that a higher up person at the client thinks my date of October 1 is totally doable! I have no idea why the timeframe has slowed down again, but I am psyched.

I cut my hair off using kitchen scissors again this morning. It looks freaky and hot. Or, rather, it will, once it calms down after having been shampooed. Right now I look like Harpo Marx.

Somehow, Cal convinced me to see Metallica, of all things, in Padova, of all places, on June 29. Then he is coming back here until July 3, when we both fly back to Paris and train down to Montpel.

Cal has a black eye. He and Victoria went to the movies and she brought in vodka and passed out and he thought she was dead and he slapped her really hard to wake her up and she awoke swinging at him reflexively.

Their world is not my world.

Chapter Twenty-One

2004-06-12

Got up at the crack of ass. Took the Eurostar first class (only seat left) DUE SOUTH. Received complimentary newspaper and snack. Gazed at passing scenery (mountains and the Med).

I arrived in Sapri over four hours later. Vincenzo picked me up and we drove up a mountain to see a statue of Christ at the top, done by the guy that did the one in Rio. The trip featured ridiculously sharp hairpin turns, and signs painted on the street for where to turn to keep ascending to see the statue that simply said CRISTO with an arrow. I found this hilarious.

Got to the top and it was indeed worth the ride. It was like looking down onto heaven. The more I see of this country, the more I am convinced that God: 1. Exists and 2. LOVES Italy.

Drove back down the mountain and went to Maratea, a lovely tiny town perched on another mountain. Walked around, had a drink at the one bar in the one piazza in Maratea. Then kept driving down to Spiaggia Nera, which was absolute paradise - hardly anyone on it; warm, clear water to swim in; a grotto with a waterfall that provided much-needed shade; and pizza and homemade wine provided by Vincenzo. It was absolute bliss.

We then took another terrifying hairpin drive back to Fardella, where his family lives. It too is a tiny lovely town perched on a mountain. We first stopped by the family farm, or fields, I guess - there are no animals. We met up with V's mom and sister, Concetta, who were transferring tomato plants. We walked through their vineyards, olive trees, apricot trees, rose bushes, and other vegetation. I saw the cantina where they make the wine, and shelves full of bottles from years past. So this is where all that delicious foodcomes from!

V's mom lives in a strangely built, multi-level apartment that is part of a bigger building, where her sisters and their husbands also live, in other strangely built apartments. Apparently their father had the whole building as one house and kept dividing it up as the daughters married. The guy who put in their steps was a drunk and, well, it shows. They're like an M.C. Escher painting. I had to ask V to guide me up the steps because it messed with my depth perception so badly.

That night we had spaghetti with mushroom sauce, because V's mom's sister found the mushrooms that day in the FAMILY FOREST and brought them over earlier. Chicken cutlets also, and fruit picked that day, and wine from the cantina. During the preparation and eating of dinner, various relatives walked by the house and stopped in, chatting and/or bringing food from their farms (fresh eggs from another sister, nectarines from someone else).

After dinner we did a passeggiata and I was given a personal Di Sanza Family Tour of Fardella - "another cousin lives here," "here is where we keep our wood," "this building is 900 years old," "my uncle used to live here." Then we got back to their street and all the sisters were outside chatting, and they held my hands and ran their hands over my cheeks and spoke in dialect and overlapped and interrupted each other and laughed and gave me tips for my sunburn, which I assured them would be brown tomorrow.

Slept in V's old attic room, with the doors open onto the balcony and lit only by starlight. Cool mountain air + total silence = slept like I was drugged.

Called out to Vincenzo to guide me down the stairs. Got cleaned up and dressed and hung out with V's sister Concetta and little daughter Anna, who is a diva in training. She has the entire family wrapped around her finger. Histrionics are her general tools of power. Children are a mystery to me.

V's mom made pasta from scratch and she taught me how to roll the pieces out with my two index fingers, and I succeeded in making all of seven pieces until she was like, OK you're done. She has a huge wooden board that she places over the sink in her tinsy kitchen, and makes it all there, putting the finished pieces on old cardboard pastry trays.

Miss Expatria

Concetta and I walked with Anna to the church in the piazza, and waited outside for the religious procession to start. She told me it was a yearly procession in honor of Jesus; I couldn't get much more of the story because she spoke such a strong dialect. The procession consisted of altar boys and the town's children carrying baskets of flower petals, the priest with town dignitaries holding a satin canopy over his head, and all the women and girls in the town. All the men sit outside the bars on the main street and watch. I don't think this is officially how it is supposed to be, but the men of Fardella aren't really the types to go walking around the whole town reciting prayers and walking on strewn flower petals.

I wanted to get a photo of it as it started and wound up walking with Concetta for the whole duration, refilling the girls' flower baskets from bags we were carrying whenever they came running back from the front of the procession. All the women chatted and gossiped and then when a lady from the church would start a prayer recitation through a megaphone, they stopped gossiping just long enough to reply "prega per noi" and then went right back to their conversations. Everyone from the town hangs their best sheets out on their balconies for this procession, finely embroidered and gleaming white; I don't know why. As the procession broke up everyone told each other buon appetito, because they all knew everyone was going home for Sunday lunch.

I then went with V and his mom to the community center around the corner, so they could vote. In the entrance they have all 72 kabillion political parties listed, with the nominees and their dates and cities of birth. The ballots are put in cardboard boxes sealed with packing tape. It did not look too official to me, but it was very exciting! Since the procession, all the men had moved from the bars to the community center and were now discussing politics. I have never wanted to know a dialect so badly as I did at that moment.

We finally made it back to the house and V's mom put Sunday lunch together. She made sure to show me that she was putting my seven sad pieces of pasta in the pot with hers. Of course when we sat down to eat, she called out all seven of my pieces, "Here's one of Christine's," because they were so sad looking. We also had all kinds of cured meats and peppers and mushrooms and olives and fruit and wine and bread.

Concetta's husband was there; he ate spaghetti that V's mom cooked for him because he doesn't like the homemades (which made me inherently distrust him), got up to go home for a nap, and never said a word. He never looked up from his plate; I was never even introduced to him. I think he knows he is outnumbered by the Di Sanza women and has learned to just shut up.

After lunch, V, his mom and I drove up to the FAMILY FOREST to look for mushrooms. I am so not cut out for country life, as was evidenced by me in large rubber boots whining at the presence of bees and relying on V's mom, who is a tiny old lady, to guide me up steep stone-filled ruts on the precipice of this mountain.

We did not find any mushrooms.

Miss Expatria

It was finally time to go to the other beach, on the other side of Italy. Well, not the other side, but the Gulf of Taranto, between Calabria and the high-heeled part of the boot of Italy. We made two pit stops - one at a REALLY REALLY OLD church that was absolutely magnificent, and completely empty except for two dogs and some beetles; and at a gas station in the MIDDLE OF NOWHERE to fill up the tank.

On the way back from the beach we stopped off at a really cool part of the Sinni river, where you can go swimming in beautifully clear water among rocks that are so big, so smooth, and so well placed that it looks like a movie set.

We also stopped at Fontana Acquafredda, a natural spring, and Vince stocked up on cold, yummy water. It's literally spring water that comes through a pipe and runs onto the ground. There are no signs or anything; it's off the side of the road under some trees. The people of Fardella know about it because they have all lived there for 500 years or more.

Back at the house we had fresh fried eggs, French fries, veal cutlets, cheese, fruit, marinated mushrooms, wine, fresh spring water.

After dinner, Concetta and Anna came over and we took another passeggiata down to another fresh spring, which was also delightfully cold and yummy. This one was more "finished," and featured enormous marble sinks with sloped sides, and a long trough. V's mom told me that this is where her mom, and all the women of Fardella, used to come to do their laundry. I cannot imagine what a pain in the ass it would be to haul your laundry down a steep hill, clean it in freezing cold water in stone and marble sinks, then haul it back up all wet and heavy; but the view was spectacular and the whole idea takes on a romantic glow when you hear V's mom talk about it in her careful, non-dialect Italian.

We walked back around to see how they were doing counting up the votes; apparently everyone else had this idea, because I think half the town was there, hanging out and talking about the votes.

Went home, was guided up the Escher steps, fell into a coma. Woke up early. Took long treacherous ride to Sapri. Took Eurostar back to the 21st century, to my home, to Rome.

There is so much I am not including in this account of my weekend:

Everyone drives Fiat Pandas, which were apparently made for rough country driving, even though they look like Yugos.

The streetlights are deliberately turned out in large parts of Fardella, so you can see the stars better.

Everyone moves at a slower pace; everyone greets each other in passing.

Anna took me on her own little tour of Fardella, avoiding barking dogs and snapping poppy leaves on our foreheads and stealing peas from a neighbor's garden.

Miss Expatria

I was in a place where I was the only stranger.

There are people in this world who live a life profoundly true and devoid of any pretense.

The strangely lush, lunar desert terrain of Basilicata.

The Hawaii smell from the yellow-flower bushes that grow wild everywhere.

I had to conjugate everything in the formal tense for V's mom and her sisters.

V and his mom observed and discussed every bird, flower, plant and orchard we passed, in this most relaxed and magical way, that when combined with the breeze through the car windows, made me drowsy and happy.

Saw kids on bikes and kicking a ball around and being KIDS, in the carefree truly youthful way my parents talk about being kids.

There was nothing precious or ORGANIC MACRO-BIOTIC SUPER DUPER HEALTHY CHI-CHI about eating delicious, fresh foods.

I watched the excited anticipation in V's aunts as they told a new person old family stories.

The only time Vincenzo ever got riled was when he realized he couldn't show me everything they wanted me to see.

The mountain air at night. The salt air in my lungs. The cool shade of the grotto, the sound of the waterfall, my eyes getting heavy from the glare of the sun on the sea.

Taking a moment to seriously ponder if maybe I had died and had gone to heaven.

2004-06-18

Work called. No go on working on new account. Am going home in November, after the elections.

I got a FedEx from work today with three reams of reports I have to go through. I am not sure exactly how I am supposed to summon the incentive to do this work.

Preliminary list of things that don't suck about moving back to New York:

Knicks games
Ess-a-bagels
New York Times that doesn't cost 6 euro

Chapter Twenty-two

2004-06-30

Monday, went to Venice. Hotel was awesome and in a great location and I will stay there every single time I go to Venice, until I somehow get rich enough to buy my own big palazzo pile and become Peggy Guggenheim reincarnated, complete with many tiny, bitchy dogs and fabulous sunglasses.

Picked up Cal from the airport. Tried to find a place to feed the poor kid, everything was closed, finally got decent pizza takeout.

(In completely unrelated news, I took the opportunity of being at Termini at a ridiculous hour this morning to have an Egg McMuffin at the only McDonald's in Rome that has them. Not at the two McDonald's in Termini, but the one across the street. Yummy fake badness. It'll hold me for another year.)

Tuesday, took a train to Padova and checked into AMAZING HOTEL. Metallica concert was AMAZING and a very chill crowd, love the Italians. Could not get a taxi after the show and walked about 186 miles back from the stadium to the hotel, got back at around 2:30AM. It was seriously like walking from Shea Stadium back to Grand Central. But we did it without a map, and talked the whole way, and actually had a lot of fun.

Today, took the train with Cal back to Rome. We are together at Romalife!

2004-07-01

Dinner at my favorite Ethiopian restaurant with Cal was a very normal evening, which for some reason will stick in my mind for the rest of my life as being one of the things that crystallized my whole experience here, and of being in my early 30s. We were two American expats in Rome, quietly sharing an exotic meal in an out of the way place, and it was so normal. It was something I never thought my life would include, in my wildest dreams.

Cal wanted to take me for a drink after, so we went to the Metropolitan Hotel and sat outside on the roof and had very elegant drinks, and the waiter remembered me from when Nicolette took me there after her tour went bust. He again complimented me on my Italian, and he wooed Cal in French.

2004-07-05

Dinner with Cal and the boys was great. Marco, Gio and Remo came over, and we all talked in several languages and laughed a lot. Cal made vodka sauce and sausages grilled in wine and the guys ate every bit of it and cleaned their plates! They were quite impressed, even though I think they don't get him at all. At least there were no awkward silences or weird vibes.

Saturday we flew/trained back to France. I like traveling with Cal - he never has any idea where he is going and is so afraid of getting lost or separated that he just lets me figure everything out, which is how I like it when I travel.

We also are addicted to train travel, so we're both on the same wavelength. Also he loves this chicken they serve on the train, and I love these brie and walnut sandwiches at Orly, so we both got to have our favorite travel food and were thoroughly content.

We had pizza from the place downstairs from his apartment; we order and then go upstairs and the waiter brings us our food! It's like having room service.

THE FALL. It's looming around us; it's a long time away, and right around the corner; it is the third person in the room.

Ugh.

2004-07-12

I miss him.

We wound up having pretty much no money between us the last couple of days, so for the most part we experimented with all the different kinds of pasta we knew how to make, watched a lot of *The West Wing* and fantasized about entering politics and argued political theory, smoked cheap French cigs, drank cheap French wine (me) and cheap German beer (him), and had the most perfect time known to mankind.

In case that wasn't being-broke-with-fabulous-boyfriend-in-the-South-of-France romantic enough, here is a tidbit to remind me that my life is a movie, and not really real, and that one's actual life cannot possibly exist in this plane:

Late Friday night I am cooking pasta and he goes to his Internet place to check on emails. He comes back 10 minutes later, holding a tiny grey kitten.

Yes, a kitten. Tiny and grey, with big blue eyes.

It fell out of a window and landed directly in front of him, and when he couldn't locate the owners, he brought him home. So we hung out with tiny grey kitten and let it share our pasta-and-*West-Wing* marathon, all of which it seemed to enjoy.

Who in real life finds an adorable, perfectly healthy, people-loving kitten at one's feet and brings it home to adoring girlfriend who is cooking delicious dinner in Southern French hovel apartment?

2004-07-23

Me: heard from mk last night
Me: she had a meeting with her boss at the new place where she works
Ma: oh tell all

Me: her boss is really excited and totally sold on the virtual thing

Me: I am meeting with them via phone next thursday

Ma: SHUT UP

Me: I have to work all weekend to get them a presentation by tuesday

Ma: SHUT UP SHUT UP SHUT UP

Me: this new boss DOES NOT WANT TO SEE ME after I initially go there to get the thing built, basically

Me: prob every 3 months or so

Ma: shut up

Me: this is going to work, mom

Me: remember the last time I said that? It was april 2002

Me: and IT WORKED

Me: and it's going to work again

Me: all the people at this new place have worked with me here, they hired up a whole bunch of them, so they have had no prob with it

Me: it's a formula for success

Me: it's going to work, I just have to be quiet about it and only me, mk and ben know that my ultimate plan is to move back here

Ma: well, my little girl, if this all comes out, it will be the coup of the century

Me: I know

Me: I will be the queen of all things

Me: I will be insufferable

Me: there will be no stopping me

Miss Expatria

2004-07-28

It's weird to date someone who lives far away when you add in the factor of IM. My relationship with Cal moves in two different tracks, at different rates. We get to know each other really well this way, just by talking all day every day, without the distraction of being face to face. Then when we see each other, can enjoy being together without the distraction of getting to know one another.

We can, for example, sit and watch 647 episodes of *West Wing* and only pause it to eat, run out for cigs, or discuss politics. There's no feeling of using the TV as a babysitter, or that we are watching it because otherwise we'd be awkwardly sitting in silence. Being able to talk to him every day makes being with him in person seem very normal and at the same time very exciting. It's a strange dynamic.

This is a strange summer, and not at all like I expected. For one, I certainly was not expecting to be dating someone who lives in France.

My life is so different than it was a year ago; so different than it will ever be again; light years away from anything I have dreamed; exactly how I knew it would be, because I willed it so.

This morning, for some reason, I looked around my room. All the books bought for me by my boyfriend at a tiny, dusty English bookshop in southern France; my favorite bags and my velvet slipper collection from Venice; PJ's of men's tank tops from the discount Roman department store;

Miss Expatria

piles of books and newspapers and magazines in three languages; Chanel nail polish and perfume and shoes, Italian suntan lotion, French mascara, Marks & Spencer underwear, a bikini thrown over the armadio door, a summer bracelet from home; a bowl of ticket stubs from the Paris metro, from plane trips to Bilbao and Paris and London, from train trips to Venice, Sapri, Sienna, Montpellier, Milan; Spanish tapas bar business cards, Indian food receipts from Montpellier, Rome and London.

This is my life as it is right now, strewn around my room; my room with impossibly high ceilings and large doors and a balcony and stone floors.

Chapter Twenty-three

2004-07-31

Sperlonga!

Yesterday we went to Sperlonga with Luca, Alfio, Daniele (Luca's friend from Verona, complete with awesome accent), and Valeria (an Argentine transsexual whose favorite phrase is "the horror," said either in French or Italian).

We all got up early and took two cars; it's about halfway between Rome and Naples. The road is very cliffy, very curvy, and there are lots of tiny places to park and cove-like beaches dotting the coast. The sea is crystal clear and has the perfect temperature. The sand is like OC sand, perfect and silky. And these places are never packed! It's incredible.

On the way down, we were treated to the sight of Alfio and Valeria in her convertible, both donning scarves and sunglasses, waving to us as they passed us.

Alfio and Luca are writing a short film and they want me to star in it as a housewife who kills her husband with kitchen scissors. I suspect this is some sort of elaborate ploy to get me to stop cutting my hair with kitchen scissors, which I do when I get an errant curl, which makes Luca crazy when it becomes his task to fix it all.

The water had a low gully and a sandbar, and it never got too deep, even pretty far out. There were some waves, which is rare for the Med in my experience, and each wave crested wolf's-eye blue before crashing; truly spectacular. Also, it is much saltier than the water to the north, so I was treated to the salty air I miss so much, and that heavy feeling in my lungs when I went to sleep last night. I love that; it reminds me of growing up at the shore.

The day was spent in and out of the sea. Luca led us in synchronized swimming routines. When one of us came back from swimming, we generally crashed directly on the sand at the water's edge. We ate the cutlets and pasta salad I made, standing up in a circle by the towels, huddling around the tupperware container and dripping wet, like little kids, eating with our hands.

They could not get over the fact that I cooked. I told them that where I come from, the Italians don't go to the beach without bringing enough food to feed an army. They found this highly amusing.

They also were amazed at how I could drink the water we had so quickly, as it was basically melted ice (we had frozen the bottles the night before). Italians have this weird thing about drinking too much water, and drinking or swimming in water that is too cold. They don't, surprisingly, have a weird thing about going back into the water right after eating.

We left the beach about 7:30, and stopped at a place on the side of the road to eat buffala mozzarella. These places are all over the coast, tiny shacks with tables where you can... well, eat mozzarella. We each got a softball-sized thing of mozz in a plastic soup bowl; they all got theirs with tomatoes and olives strewn over the top, and I got mine with sun-dried tomatoes. We got some loaves of bread and bottles of water and sat down at one of the picnic tables directly on the edge of the cliff, and ate and watched the sun sink into the Med.

On the way back in the car we played guessing games and word games and sang along to Sheryl Crow songs. Marco and I got home at about 11:30, took showers, and PASSED OUT. I don't think I have had a day like that, at the beach running in and out of the water and eating standing up and laughing, since I was about nine years old. It was awesome.

2004-07-31

The new job meeting went spectacularly well. They were blown away. The highlight, however, was:

"Do you really need to move back to the US? I mean, we really don't care if you work from Italy or not."

Let the games begin.

2004-08-02

I woke up today to a different Rome. It is COMPLETELY EMPTY, except for 14 sweaty German tourists. It's absolute bliss.

It's ridiculously quiet; so many shutters are closed; restaurants and stores have their grates down; there's nothing to do but walk down the middle of the street eating ice cream and then smoke cigarettes on the stoop across the street from work, where the shade is.

You also get a true sense of the differences from neighborhood to neighborhood, from piazza to piazza, because there's nothing in between to distract you. You're completely alone on a street, then you come upon a piazza and see a snapshot of that neighborhood's life, and then you pass through and it's gone.

Sylvietta, the neighborhood cat, has taken to sleeping under cars next to the rear wheels.

2004-08-11

Of all the madcap, fabulous, glamorous things I have done since I've lived here, meeting Cal in Paris this weekend is definitely the most madcap, most fabulous, most glamorous thing of them all. Especially since we have the same ideas about how the weekend should go, and it was not the typical "weekend in Paris with one's boyfriend" weekend.

He took the train from Montpel. I flew in from Rome. I showed up at Gare de Lyon as his train pulled in. I love good timing.

Miss Expatria

He brought me another Ellroy book. He has made a ritual of meeting me at train stations and airports all over Europe and presenting me with a new book during that first moment and it just, it devastates me. It crushes me. It is by far the romantic thing any man has ever done for me.

Planet Hollywood on the Champs Elysees: Two expats in great need of American food, drinks with ice cubes in them, and air conditioning. He had chicken fingers and a bacon cheeseburger, I had a cheesesteak and a brownie, and we discussed the 2nd Amendment.

He took me past the crepe cart he ate at every single day when when he was 14; although he's American, he was born in Paris and his father regularly shipped him off to Paris to keep in touch with it, more or less.

I showed him the exact place right in front of the St. Michel Metro stop where, as I was leaving for the airport after New Year's 2000, I made the decision to live in Europe at any cost.

Saturday and Sunday mornings were similar to each other: Long mornings in the room, which had a private courtyard, eating room service breakfast and old New York Times Sunday magazines that Rich had brought me. Sometimes we talked a lot, and sometimes we were silent. We watched CNN obsessively, and realized it was the first time either of us had heard John Kerry speak or seen him move.

Monday morning my alarm went off and as I went to grab it, he pulled me towards him and held me so tight and said,

Miss Expatria

"Never leave" and I could feel his breath on my neck as he said it. But leave him I did, standing alone and in tears in the hotel room, and I dropped my bag and hugged him and told him we'll see each other in Barcelona in less than a month.

Chapter Twenty-four

2004-08-16

I met Howie my first day at college. In another life, we'd be married and have six kids; in this one, we're just friends and thick as thieves. We've watched each other grow up into a couple of amazing adults, and we cheer each other on and vow to avenge anyone who has done the other wrong.

When the World Trade Center was bombed the first time, Howie was working at CNN and stayed on the phone with me as he read what was coming off the wires. He was the first person I called, incoherent and sobbing, when my father had a heart attack; Howie was at my door four minuts later. He is my rock.

And now, finally, my dear darling Howie is here on vacation. We had a magical day! Vincenzo took us for a drive to the San Sebastiano catacombe - my first and DEFINITELY LAST time in a catacombe. A little too cramped, but a nice thing to do on a hot day.

Then we drove down the Appia Antica, backtracked and went along the aquaducts, and had a picnic prepared entirely by Vincenzo's mom: Roasted peppers stuffed with bread, anchovies and olive oil, zucchine slices topped with meatballs, cheese, fruit, bread, homemade wine.

There seems to be no languge barrier between Howie and the gay mafia; somehow, with only a little bit of translating from me, they seem to understand each other.

2004-08-20

There are three islands in the Bay of Naples - Capri, Ischia, and Procida. Everyone goes to Capri and Ischia. There are no tourists on Procida; only hard-core Italians who obviously go there every year. Not a word of any other language spoken that I heard, no one with cameras, no one with maps. Procida. La Casa sul Mare hotel. Only trip to take, EVER. Forget Ischia and Capri. Viva Procida!

Vincenzo's boyfriend Salvatore met us at the train station in Naples and took us to the ferry docks. He had his tiny work car, so he could only take one of us at a time. I let Howie go first, since the Naples train station is SUCH a hellhole.

We took a taxi up and down several hills on Procida to our hotel. Ten rooms, all with private, enormous terraces facing the cove. We took a walk down to the promenade in the cove and ate lunch outside under umbrellas next to the small fishing boats docked there, alongside families in bathing suits. Everyone was salty and beachified.

Procida, I can't explain it - it's not pretentious, it's not touristy, it's just the most perfect place ever. The main port we came into was busy with motorinos and cars and people and big ferries. Our port, on the other side of the island, had no motor traffic, and only little dinghies and fishing boats came in and out. Tremendously slow paced, everyone very tan and the sea is a part of their lives, not in a rugged way, but you can see the sea present in each person you encounter - the children are all in bathing suits all day, everyone is very casual, just perfect.

Howie took a walk down to the other, busier port while I worked a bit. Then we went back to the same place for dinner, because at lunch we saw a huge table of people eating spaghetti with mussels, and we decided that had to be our dinner.

We had enormous bruschette with eggplant and tomatoes and mozzarella and tuna, and the spags with mussels, and white wine, and soaked up all the delicious briny garlicky oil with more bread than two people should be able to consume. We were there for three hours, outside in the night air, tranquil, water lapping, smoking cigs and drinking and talking nonstop about everything, it was like we were floating in the water. And the mussels tasted like tiny pats of briny, garlicky butter - we joked about not knowing that butter grew in the sea. They literally melted in our mouths.

We slept like two dead people and in the morning we had breakfast delivered to the room on the terrace, an enormous tray of pastries and fruit. Took the noon "boat" (tiny dinghy) to the beach across the cove. Several kids who are obviously friends with the boat guy all jumped in as well, all laughing and joking with the boat guy.

Miss Expatria

It was the first time I had ever wanted to be eight years old again, with nothing to do all day but stay in my bathing suit and be salty and tan and go back and forth on a small boat with my friends.

Swam in crystal clear, limpid, warm water, collapsed on our towels, watched the comings and goings of absolutely everyone, chatted, slept, read, heaven.

Took the boat back at 4ish, showered, worked a bit, bought wine at a market and drank the whole thing on the terrace while watching the sun set over Ischia's hills in the distance. Went to the same place for dinner and had the same exact meal, but with more wine. Three hours of eating, sighing, yumming, talking, laughing.

Next day, more blissful beach sun sea lovely air jellyfish are called medusas laughing relaxing into oblivion, then dinner at a terraced restaurant perched on a close-by hill we could see from our room. Calamari, antipasto, linguine with mixed seafood, spaghetti with swordfish and eggplant. Wine. Bread. A chocolate semifreddo that I thought was going to make Howie pass out. Went back to the room and listened to a whole bunch of music on my computer on the terrace, smoking and talking and laughing and sometimes being serious.

Back to Rome. He took us all out for dinner! Then later that night me, Howie, Marco, Vincenzo, and gay Enzo (they're all gay, but "gay Enzo" differentiates him from Salvatore's hot cousin Enzo, who is blessedly straight) all climbed in Vince's car and drove out to some natural hot springs near Viterbo.

Miss Expatria

There are three baths there, of varying temperatures, out in the middle of a field, off an unmarked dirt road, completely unlit except by the almost-full moon; groups of friends all floating and chatting, just moonlight and water and splashing and laughing and we stayed there for about three hours, skin like prunes and soft from the sulfur and the night air was fresh and chilly.

Then we all climbed back in the car and drove Howie directly to the airport, stopping for fresh pastry along the way, and got him there at 5:30, just in time for him to check in for his 7AM flight. We watched the sun slowly rise as we drove east back to Rome, and Marco and I crawled into our beds just as the streetlights went off for the day.

2004-09-07

Barcelona, where the winds all blew!

Being expats in need of American food, Cal and I ate at the Hard Rock Cafe much too often (BUT OH! OH! ROAST BEEF SANDWICH WITH CHEDDAR CHEESE ON PUMPERNICKEL BREAD AND A PEANUT BUTTER CHOCOLATE BROWNIE THING!), had bagels every morning at what has to be the best bagel place east of New York, ate yummy tapas, saw Gaudi stuff.

Miss Expatria

Random:

- Finding a really cool, upscale tapas place and sitting at the bar and feeling very chic
- La Rambla seriously sucks; sweaty English tourists with enormous beers
- Going in everyday to the slot machine place and putting in one euro and pushing all the buttons, and one time we won 2.40 euro and didn't know why
- BAGELS OMG
- Waking up on Monday to an enormous cruiseship smokestack directly outside our window
- Hanging out in our swanky hotel room in oversized cushy white hotel robes and watching CNN and becoming reacquainted with air conditioning
- Laughing about how Bush made his big nomination speech and because of the Russian horror and Clinton's bypass, it got NO AIRTIME
- Watching a Larry King rerun of his most recent Clinton interview and just staring, transfixed at the awesomeness that is Clinton, and just plain wanting him to be our president again

2004-10-11

Ben, who is divine and one of my closest friends, came to Rome, totally randomly! He is yet another agency alum who has gone on to work at the new place, so we gossiped about coworkers and got all excited about my chances of working with everyone again and continuing to live in Rome.

Miss Expatria

We spent two days in Rome, ate good food, hung out. Went with Giovanni to dinner at Tram Tram, where Gio and I learned he is voting for Bush for reasons we still cannot understand. Apparently, Gio immediately went and told everyone in a horrified manner of Ben's voting choice, and now they are all scandalized and making fun of me for being friends with him. I love my gay mafia.

Monday we went to Venice. On the train they make a recorded announcement in Italian and English about the stops it makes, where the bar and restaurant cars are, where the conductor is located, etc. In English they say Train Guard, but with the severe British accent it sounds like Train God.

Venice. It was the best time I have had there, due to Ben's insane generosity. We ate unbelievable cichetti for every meal, walked around, took the grand canal boat like a hundred times, and had way too many drinks at Florian in Piazza San Marco.

It was his first time in Venice, and the piazza looks so lovely at night - so when we got off the boat, I made him close his eyes and I led him to the middle of the piazza. He opened them, stared in amazement, and promptly thanked me for one of the top ten moments of his life.

On Wednesday we took the train to Firenze and then to S. Ellero, where Famous Jimmy met us and took us to his rented villa in Donnini. Gorgeous. Jimmy is also generous to a fault - we did not have to lift a finger for anything we needed, or even remotely dreamed of. Ben had his own room in the guest wing, and I had my own APARTMENT down by the pool.

Jimmy served us their previous night's leftovers for lunch - pork marinated in wine, cheeses, olives, polenta drizzled with white truffle oil, peaches, really good bread, really good wine.

We took a drive to a vineyard owned by a friend of Famous Jimmy's - Jimmy's the kind of guy who knows people who own vineyards in Tuscany - and watched them destemming the day's pick in a huge machine that we had to climb up and look into. The building connected to the vineyard was a big old pile of delicious, crumbling palazzo, with a beautiful tasting room.

Ben and Jimmy went to a dinner/tasting there that night, while Fran and I went into Florence and walked around a bit, and then drank a really good bottle of wine in an outdoor place in a huge piazza. We took a taxi back to Donnini and I proceeded to have one of the top ten sleeps of my life.

The next day we got up and went to Villa Pitiana, a hotel and restaurant owned by more wine freaks that Famous Jimmy has met over the years. It was breathtakingly beautiful. The owner let me get some quick work done on the computer in his office, and then his secretary called Famous Jimmy for me when I was done.

He, Fran and Ben were in the next town over and had just ordered lunch. He came and got me and we sat down to five pastas - Bolognese, coniglie ragu, pesto, lemon ravioli, and bottarga. Another amazing bottle of wine. REALLY spectacular lunch in this tiny osteria that was the only restaurant in the whole town.

As we walked out, we saw a woman who was walking with an old man up the street. He obviously had dimentia; he was screaming for help and so plainly confused and scared. It was heartbreaking.

We took a long and nausea-inducing ride up through some hills to try to find a place that Ben remembers from a family trip; took power naps back at the house; then it was time for dinner in Florence at a place called Cibreo, which apparently is a mecca for food freaks - and rightly so. There were seven of us - Jimmy and Fran; me and Ben; Benedetta, who runs a clothing store that Jimmy loves; and Roberta and Errol, who used to be Jimmy's neighbors in New York. I had porcini mushroom passata and lamb's brains cooked in butter. We all tried each other's dishes. The chef came over and made fun of me for putting so many pieces of bread in my butter sauce.

There was not one thing I did not absolutely faint over. It was the most consistently good meal I think I have ever had. We ordered every dessert off the menu, and passed the plates after every bite. We changed wines for each course and had wine beforehand and digestivi afterwards. It was absolute gluttony; marvelous and surprisingly unpretentious.

We took a taxi back to the hills, picked up the car, and went back to Villa Pitiana, where Stefano, Roberto and Marco busted open some wines we just HAD to try. They did the whole thing where they take the first few drops of wine and swirl a bit in each glass before decanting the rest. We had to taste it, then wait a bit and taste it again. And WOW did these wines change taste! It was really amazing. Especially since the wine I drink most often costs 1.85 euro at the discount supermarket.

Famous Jimmy has been coming to Donnini for about 10 years. He introduced me and Ben to random people in the town; when I spoke to them in Italian and it was obvious to them I was fluent, they would all ask me to ask Jimmy a question that they have always wanted to know or that they have tried to ask him but he did not understand well enough to answer. Which is not surprising; they all spoke some mean Tuscan dialect up in those hills – a perfect example: Coca Cola is pronounced *Hoha Hola*.

The bar lady asked me to ask him how to reheat the sausage bread he gave her. Tosca the maid asked all kinds of household questions. The baker wanted me to tell Jimmy they had a fire last year. I was called in every direction to translate something for Italians who wanted so much to talk with *Jee-mee*.

2004-10-15

I booked my ticket back to the States. November 8, I land at JFK. Now, I just need a job! They still haven't come back to me about hthe new job - they keep telling MK and Ben that they're interested, and they want to meet with me when I get back. Come ON, people.

Miss Expatria

2004-10-23

Last night I dreamt in Italian, and for the first time, it was not a dream in which I was struggling with the language, and it was not a dream that featured any of my friends here. I was at some kind of villa, on vacation, with a family, and it was just in general a banal dream, but when I awoke I was thinking completely in Italian; it took me a moment to realize I had another language roaming around in my head. I kind of felt like Jason Bourne for a minute.

For the first time last night, I wondered where this whole thing is going with Cal, and it hit me like a ton of bricks. This is unlike any relationship have ever been in, and it frankly scares me, and I mean that in the best possible way. What we have is so flawed and powerful and amazing, and it is so precious to me. Every day brings something new and wonderful. It's magic.

2004-10-27

A German student named Christoph is taking my room for however long I am away. That is a huge load off of my shoulders, since paying 135 is better than paying 485 (I am paying the balance of what he cannot afford in order to keep control over the room, long boring story).

Heard from Cal this morning - he and his brother, who was in Montpel on vacation, were stuck at the train station because there was a dead body on the train. They didn't get on the way to Barcelona until 10AM (instead of 6:30AM). His life is so strangely eventful.

Miss Expatria

2004-10-28

Marco and I decided to leave work early. We went to the grase truck by Porta Maggiore and had the best sausage sandwiches ever. It's run by this old lady, her daughter and some other guy. The old lady works the register. She had green fingernail polish and did everything with a cigarette hanging out of her mouth, taking her own sweet time, and there's nothing you can do about it but marvel at her fabulousness. It was worth the wait, for the entire experience.

2004-10-29

On the way home from running an errand, I took the tram to the Colosseum and walked to work because there were Carabinieri everywhere, Piazza Venezia was closed, everything was a mess.

Turns out, 15 heads of state were at Piazza Venezia signing the new European constitution. I mentioned it to Vincenzo, and he said, "Always remember you were in Rome for this historic day."

I will, Vincenzo. I will. How could I ever forget?

2004-10-31

My last day in Rome.

On the way home, Marco and I had to walk to the tram because Fori Imperiale was closed, and we stopped in at a bar and had tramezzini and prosecco and watched an awesome rainstorm come screaming over the Colosseum - ominous, powerful, and just for us. Then we came home and my cousin Louis was there - he popped over again to see me before I left, he kills me - and had already bought stuff to make our grandmother's chicken. I think Viola greeted him at the door demanding that he make it for her.

Luca is coming over to give me Ansiolin (liquid Valium; don't fly without it) and cut my hair; Louis is thrilled to see him in action. Vincenzo might stop by. Gio is no doubt coming over to play cards. More wine will be drunk. Marco will make miracles out of whatever is in our kitchen.

My last day in Rome.

2004-11-02

I woke up before dawn on Monday; I left without saying goodbye. I couldn't face them. I rode the train out to the airport, and saw that the sun had in fact risen on this day, and I knew there was no choice but to start a new phase of my life.

And the fog lifting through the fields, and the smell of the hundreds of espressos being made all throughout the airport, and the funny, lyrical conversations which only two years ago were senseless to my ears.

My plane did not crash. My train did not derail. And as I came out of the station in Montpellier, there he was.

The rest of my day is dedicated to laundry, backgammon, checking into the hotel with CNN down the street, taking a bath in an actual tub, and watching the elections.

Nothing else matters.

2004-11-03

I cannot believe this is happening. Has America become some third world country? If I were the EU, I would get every country to sign a petition getting the UN involved in election monitoring. What is so hard about counting votes? Bush is going to win this thing, and we're in some serious shit after that. Europe is in shock. It's not even funny. I can't get back here fast enough.

I am outraged.

This is not coming out right. I'm sorry if this sounds like anti-American rhetoric. It's not. I'm just sick of America right now.

Chapter Twenty-five

2004-11-12

That strange feeling is not election hangover. It's my presence in the United States.

To recap:

Sunday, last day in Europe. Brunch at Lu and Mu's. Backgammon all day at the big table at the pub, everyone hanging out with us at one time or another, having great, funny conversations and an amazing, fun afternoon.

Next morning, silent walk to the train station. He told me not to forget him. As if.

Lufthansa staff on strike in Paris, which worked to my advantage - wound up literally checking in and walking directly onto each flight, in Paris and in Frankfurt.

Even with Ansiolin and wine, I cried for eight straight hours. It started when I walked up to the gate and there was a flight to Heathrow across the corridor, and as I was looking at it, they called the flight to New York. It was really happening and I could do nothing to stop it. I could not stop the tears, so I just let them come.

I was the first person through customs, immigration and out the door. Saw MK and Jax, who had come to pick me up, and really, really started sobbing. It was such a release of every emotion I have felt in the last two years! The defining era of my entire adult life had come to an end in JFK airport, where it all started.

I will go back. I will live in Europe for the rest of my life, somehow. But it will never be like this first time. It's over.

Next day, in PJs all day, hanging with Mom. Had her gravy and meatballs for dinner. Yesterday, shopping errands - Dollar Store, Payless Shoes, Sears, Best Buy, all the crazy huge American stores and all those aisles of stuff. Lunch at Applebee's, at the bar so we could smoke. Today, the cable guy is coming to hook up wireless cable Internet.

Many phonecalls and messages to Cal, much IMing him, we are still connected, to my great relief. The bond is still so strong it makes me weak.

I am really surprised at the amount of culture shock I had. I think it is because I had simply accepted my life in Rome; as magical as it always was, the novelty had worn off and it simply became my life.

2004-11-17

The TV never goes off. The heat is always on too high. Commercials are edited weirdly. My parents right now are asleep on the sofas. There's some shitting sports review show on, and they are incessantly talking about some NFL commercial with Terrell Owens and Nicolette Sheridan. If I hear the word "Fallujah" one more time I am starting my own jihad. I need a winter coat.

2004-11-23

Went to NYC, had to stop in and bring the laptop back. People at my old work were more than happy to see me, which was weird - they stopped in their tracks and were like, YOU LOOK STUNNING. I mean, I have lost weight, but they insisted it was something else about me.

These stupid bosses at this new place keeps hemming and hawing about giving me A FRICKING JOB. I called Fabulous Ex-Boss Orlann and she promptly offered me a huge job, then almost cried when I told her that I would only take a job with her if it was virtual, and whoever offered me a virtual job first would get me.

We went to the Roger Williams Hotel bar with her coworker Christine and had a bottle of wine and some really fun conversations, I laughed a lot. Then Famous Jimmy called and said, what are you guys doing, let's go to dinner. At 9PM on a Friday night he calls the owner of Artisinal and asks for a table for five in five minutes. We were promptly whisked into the packed restaurant to a fab table. We had oysters and a cheese plate from HEAVEN and many bottles of Barolo and then Jax came and we had several desserts and Adam, another Orlann coworker, was there and he had a bat as a pet once, he's Polish and we had the best, bitchiest, New York evening ever.

Sunday, took the bus to Mount Laurel and went to Aunt Dot's. She's the head of our family and an audience with her is necessary for major things, like returning from the homeland. Matthew and my parents showed up and we had polenta and cousin Louis showed up too and it was a typical loud meal. I really enjoyed myself.

Then my parents and Louis and I went to Aunt Ida and Uncle Ralph's and they look great for being almost 90, and their little apartment is lovely and we all yelled because they are practically deaf and had to repeat ourselves often because they also don't pay attention.

Today my grandparents come and it will be a whirlwind of activity and more yelling, because they also can't hear or pay attention. I'll be so so so happy to see them - I have a huge fear all the time that all these amazing, beautiful, old people in my family will die before I get to see them, so I am glad they all hung on until I got home. Although they are all so active and awesome, I suspect they will outlive us all.

2004-11-25

"God, I love you. The more I realize how my life is stagnant here, the more I think you and I should just find a new place, in Rome or Barcelona, anywhere but here, and live there when you come back.

You are what I am giving thanks for.

Cal"

Miss Expatria

2004-11-30

I have a ticket TO Paris, which was the second half of my ticket to the States, on Dec. 27. I want to spend New Year's with Cal. But I have no money to buy another round trip ticket back.

Am panicking about getting a fricking job. My mom gave me a huge lecture about my being irresponsible and health insurance and credit cards and school loans and all manner of adult concerns that completely invalidated the last two years of my life. It was humiliating.

Will call the new place tomorrow; called Orlann today, telling her to get me a job that's virtual. So I have all of my half-assed bases covered.

2005-01-04

It is a new year.

I finagled a return ticket from a friend with an insane amount of frequent flyer miles - am hanging out with Cal, playing backgammon, watching DVDs, making creative dinners, talking, living in ignorant bliss.

2005-01-09

On the flight on the way home, I saw the aurora borealis. It was beautiful and magical. It was a perfect ending to a beautiful and magical year.

Chapter Twenty-six

2005-01-11

My first day of work yesterday - with Fabulous Ex-Boss Orlann. The other place was just taking too long.

Slid directly down the learning curve of this new job. It seems a bit unwieldy right now. But I have a Powerbook G4 and my workspace is full of light from enormous windows and I have a spectacular view of the Empire State Building. The entire office space is beautiful, big loft high ceilings open spaces funky people music laughter real glasses in the kitchen.

Pavlov Memento called. His dad died. No one knows how, apparently. They're doing an autopsy today.

2005-02-23

Right now I am living my life as if my normally scheduled life is on hold, and this is not really real. I have taken many chances, done many stupid and/or fun things, and behaved in general like I shouldn't for the better part of two months. I have been living with no regard for anything. I feel like my life is about to end and I've thrown all caution to the wind. I am having near illegal amounts of fun, but the jury is still out on whether I will look back on this era as one of extreme darkness or extreme light. All I know is: I want to get back to my real life.

My typical day goes like this:

Wake up around 8:30. Lay in bed for 15 minutes, remembering the hilarious fun things done/said the night before.

Get up, take a quick shower; wear something I have most likely worn in the past few days, because I have not gotten around to buying a full wardrobe yet.

Brave mostly shitty weather during my annoying commute with a million other people on the L train, 90 percent of whom all look the same age and are too hip and are all listening to iPods, the other 10 percent of whom are Polish construction workers.

Get to work 25-75 minutes later, armed with a quart of Tropicana No Pulp OJ. Try to focus my eyes on a 1700-row, 46-column spreadsheet; yell at my team, who has no idea how to create a paper trail; IM Cal; get cheap Indian food for lunch.

Afternoon is spent being able to form full sentences and texting Shawn and Jeremy about what we're doing that night.

Leave work promptly at 5PM; wait for Shawn and Jeremy to come get me in my one-room, ceiling-lit, basement hovel apartment generously loaned to me by Jeremy. Go across the street and kick Shay's steel door until he comes out, then go to Daddy's, Pete's or R Bar and make each other laugh and play songs on the jukebox and all of a sudden it's 2AM and we're eating Anytime takeout lamb burgers and crying laughing and then someone says, we gotta go home.

Fall into bed. Rinse and repeat.

Went to brunch with Howie, Rich and Jax and BILL CLINTON WALKED IN. I have never seen an entire room of New Yorkers stop breathing like that. He is a force of nature. He is such a rock star.

Cal sent me 20 blood red French tulips for Valentine's Day and HE IS COMING HERE FOR TWO WEEKS.

Apparently in the last month, he has realized he cannot live without me and wants to meet my parents and has all of a sudden become sane and responsible and stuff. It's freaky and exciting and scary and I have never been so in love as I am at this moment in my life. All other love has been a joke. We found each other through each other and have learned and grown and we know where we want our lives to go and we want to get there together, side by side.

2005-03-10

This hangover is bringing me to my knees.

2005-03-15

Cal is here. I have a split lip from ripping a cig out of my mouth while my lips were dry (so classy), and I just got a cold. No plans for tonight.

2005-03-21

Ken offered me six figures to stay in NYC and do this job. I am still trying to make this job virtual. Am really, really confused, scared and excited.

Cal changed his ticket and is now staying til the 5th of April, and is coming back May 4. We have a lot to talk about and figure out. Am really, really confused, scared and excited.

2005-04-08

Cal left. I turned down the six-figure job; Ken gave me a raise to stay on as a freelancer.

I wound up at a Russian Mob strip club in Long Island City last night with my Brooklyn crew. It seemed like a good idea at the time ("the time" being 2:30AM). They are the devil.

2005-05-13

Cal is back! He has now flown across the ocean twice to see me. And is staying until I can leave. Apparently, he went back to Montpel and was so effing miserable without me that he couldn't take it anymore. Love!

Miss Expatria

I am so homesick for Rome. I miss it with all my heart. I want to go back on the next plane and marry Cal and work in a tiny bookstore. I hate this New York fast track high-speed crap.

It all is just so loud and I'm not listening to myself, my inner self. I can't hear myself anymore, I have no inner guidance, and I feel like I have sold my soul. I need some quiet, I need my fountain in my sunny piazza, I need long slow meals, I need high ceilings, I am not supposed to be living this life right now and it makes my heart burst into a million pieces that Cal has chosen to temporarily give up the life we both want to be with me.

Oh, love love love.

2005-06-20

I had a panic attack about everything. How I do not feel like myself here. How it scares me that I really don't care about seeing anyone ever again. I am in a bad way here and I don't like myself here. I have changed. I have become one of those people that drops off the face of the earth and lives far away, but I am also the person who has close ties with family and lifelong friends I would die for.

It's been a tough go.

I've been dreaming in Italian, I've been back there in my dreams and it's lovely.

Miss Expatria

Weatherwise, it's such a groovy day. If you can use some exotic booze, there's a bar in far Bombay. Come on, fly with me, let's fly, we'll fly away.

2005-07-27

Yesterday, Cal kidnapped me in his Dad's car and took me up to his family's estate in New Hampshire. It's on a thousand acres that George Washington gave to one of his ancestors as payment for fighting in the war. Not the one about whom there is a book written by William Safire, but one of his brothers? Incredible.

There is no one around; it's just us and I am never happier than when I am alone with him. We just started cocktail hour; I am having a vodka gimlet and he is having a gin martini.

Today was the first day I worked virtually with this job. This is going to happen. I am actually going to be able to do this.

Oh God, I am so happy. I really am the amazing person I know myself to be. New York drains me; I am less than human there, I am feral, I need to push my way onto the train and walk fast and sit in dull meetings and I hate it.

I have my soul back. I have missed myself so much. I feel like I found myself again. And I have been here for less than 24 hours.

Miss Expatria

2005-07-31

This week was heaven. Silent days and nights on this magnificent, enormous estate, watching the sun set every night over the mountains; eating lobster for dinner two nights in a row; going to the private beach and standing in limpid, crystal clear water and finishing a book as baby bass swam around me and Cal fed Cheetos to the ducks; having proper cocktails on the terrace promptly at 5PM; setting up a jigsaw puzzle in the dining room; hitting golf balls all over the great back lawn; having drinks on Frank Nedeau's back porch up the road and soaking in his fabulous Yankee accent; exploring JoJo's General Store and buying sparklers and poppers and balsam wood airplanes; skulking around the graveyard and the foundations of the old barn and servants' quarters on the property; and most importantly, BEING ABLE TO WORK VIRTUALLY.

This is really going to happen. I can't believe it. I feel like I can finally let myself think of life after New York. My life is going to start again.

This is a different kind of feeling than I have had before. It's not that flying feeling, that feeling that I can do anything. This is a quieter feeling, more of a confirmation of what I was always too scared to let myself dream of - that I still am right about the way I want to live my life, surrounded by beauty and not cubicles, working hard every day to make living life the priority and working simply being the means to do so.

Chapter Twenty-seven

2005-08-12

My company is letting me go virtual.

We leave mid-September.

I did it.

2005-08-22

I'm at my parents' house. Back in the room I grew up in. My mom recently redid it during some very excrutiating and marriage-trying weeks. It looks really good. It looks different.

The whole house looks different. It's not the house I see when I dream of this house. The house I dream of has brown paneling and orange carpet and hellatious floral couches. In my dreams, my room has white paneling and lime green carpet and my theater posters, and my stuffed animals hanging from the ceiling so they didn't get moldy, and my old desk and my secret hiding places.

Miss Expatria

Now the whole house is all white, and airy, and there are artfully placed shells and a model sailboat on the mantle. I wouldn't want to go back to the brown and orange. But to this day, just now in fact when we came home from Aunt Janet's, where we were sitting around the table, telling old stories and new ones and laughing, eating strawberries in triple sec and Boston cream pie; when I come back from times like those, I am always surprised by how the house looks.

I want to go to the storage facility while I am here, to where my stuff is. The stuff that used to define me. There is some stuff from this old house in there. My Hello Kitty message box, my beloved books, my mother's silver serving plates, my champagne flute collection, my old journals filed with hate and desperation, some well written or otherwise amusing college papers, all my old address books and datebooks, two American flags, a tiny saluting John John statue, a travel bar collection, and a bunch of other stuff that at one time I thought was too important to throw out. We did throw a lot of stuff out. There's still a lot of stuff left.

I wonder about that stuff all the time. I miss some of it. I miss a book by Bruce Weber of photos of Sam Shepard and Jessica Lange that I stole from the Cooper Union library. I miss a bunch of my books. The rest of the stuff I keep because it is a part of me and my history and my family's history. But what am I going to do with it - ship it to Montpel? Rome? Barcelona?? I don't want to live in one place for the rest of my life, surrounded by stuff.

Miss Expatria

So I guess for now, I'm paying $1200 a year towards something I hope one day someone will find as fascinating as my uncle Eugene's bottom drawer in his old room in my grandparents' house, filled with magic tricks and foreign coins and an old watch and high school love notes.

2005-08-26

I think on the plane on the way over it will all hit me and I'll laugh and laugh and laugh all the way, just like I cried and cried and cried from Frankfurt to JFK on November 8.

I miss beauty. I miss my gay mafia. I miss latte macchiatos. I miss tobacco shops. I miss the rhythm of my life. I miss home. I miss stone floors. I miss smoking in bars and restaurants and baggage claims. I miss the sensuality of daily life. I miss being fabulous and glamorous. I miss being anonymous. I miss speaking in the language I feel most comfortable in. I miss the IHT. I miss tramezzini. I miss coins in my pocket. I miss Fortuna Blues. I miss being unavailable and far away.

I miss expatria.

My mom still fixes my hair and checks over my clothes before I go out of the house. I'm 34 years old and feel like I am a constant source of aesthetic disappointment to her.

2005-09-01

We bought the tickets last night. We're leaving September 19.

We're leaving. We're really going back. I did it. I DID IT! I did this. I made this happen. It's really starting to hit me.

I'm not out of the woods yet - it will hit me hard this weekend, when I sit down and plan my exit strategy - appointments, dates, tasks, etc.

I love this part.

I did it. It's all I can think about.

2005-09-02

Email from Luca:

"We are waiting for you!

Gay kisses all over you

Luca Lennon & Alfio Ono"

2005-09-05

This has been such a long weekend, each day stretching out at Cal's parents' house, sans parents. Yesterday, I spent almost the entire day in the pool. Then we grilled; scallops for me and steak for him. I fell asleep on the couch, early. It was a lazy day and absolutely perfect.

This morning I woke up in the early hours and I could feel the air through the window next to the bed. It was that morning air that is still so evocative for me of visiting

Europe (as opposed to living there). It's how the air feels when it's your last morning and you have to get up at the crack of ass because all flights to the U.S. leave early. There's the sad truth that you're ending your trip and everyone else is beginning their day, and it hits you that their day will go on there, that they get to live there and you don't.

You see shopkeepers sweeping in front of their stores (yes, you really do) and you hear espresso machines gurgling and you hear plates clanking and maybe a baby crying and the light is always the saddest, because you always go as summer turns to fall and it's that sad, sad light that slants in that melancholy way that bathes everything in totally fake-looking golden light.

And you begin planning the biggest move of your life.

2005-09-09

Things I can't wait for in Montpel:

- Indian food
- Fondue
- Backgammon for HOURS with dirty expats
- Waking up when I want
- Going to bed when I want
- Decent, cheap cigarettes
- Being so close to my gay mafia
- Being anonymous again
- Not being in an office

YAY

Miss Expatria

2005-09-12

It's all starting to come together. I am sleeping better, dreaming more fantastically (flying dreams!), and "plate of shrimp" moments are happening with stunning frequency. It feels more like my life before, like my real life.

Last night, Cal said that he had a great summer here. It made my heart ache with tenderness for him as he listed all the things he liked about being here this summer - they were simple times and things that were, in retrospect, fun.

It also made me realize that he is solely responsible for the good times I have had this summer - the Bronx Zoo, New Hampshire, Bradley Beach, the empty house, movies, all of it. He is a big reason why I have made it through, and am getting back to my real life in exactly one week.

How did he do that so quietly, without the whistles, horns and bells that usually surround someone singlehandedly saving another?

There are times I think he is selfish and pays no attention to me or his surroundings - but then it is moments like last night when I am reminded with the abruptness of a 2x4 to the head that he is keenly, scarily aware, and that he knows exactly what makes me tick.

Sometimes we don't speak and it's lovely. Sometimes we can't shut up and it's fun. This morning he said to me, "We're like two puzzle pieces that fit." It's true.

2005-09-13

Went out with Jax last night, to Bubby's, and then walked up through TriBeCa and SoHo to Bleecker.

I really love that walk; I used to do it all the time with my old roommates when we lived down there. There are so many shops to browse in, and great people watching. It was a very satisfying night doing that walk with my beloved Jax, chatting nonstop and looking at bright shiny things.

But everything has changed down there. I walk around like the crazy old bag lady who only sees the New York of her past - Burrito Bar is closed, El Teddy's is knocked down, there are ridiculously expensive shops all along Franklin Street; my city is gone. It is in the pages of my diaries, in my old photos, in my memories.

2005-09-14

Here is the ticker tape in my head:

Work late today, then see Cyn at 7 Buy packing tape Steal tape gun from work Work til noon tomorrow, go home and pack Call fedex to see what they need on the boxes for customs Get fedex forms from the mail place on Graham Get fedex number from Yira Buy plug adapters Gifts for Vic, Soph, Alex Process check and get euros for Jonty Cancel phone Renew storage insurance Send all addresses to Mom Call loan people Do moving thing at status on Thursday Katie for sushi Thursday, then b&B with Tim and Cal Buy suitcase? Or no? I think no, I'll know after I pack

Install AOL on my laptop HSBC Insurance to mom Have Steve look over my computer Accountant! Oh god the acccountant, when am I going to do that, ooooohhhhh Saturday with the boys, hope that goes OK Sunday where are we going, ask Cal about time frame Saturday need to do rest of shopping and Cal buy clothes, jacket (HM, Gap, Club M) Get plan together for Kim How am I calling in to status on Tuesday? Get SIM on Wednesday, why can't I get it on Tuesday? I hope I get my period soon Need to buy more deodorant and hair shit UGH Clean apartment, Sunday and Monday? Wash sheets and towels, kitchen, floor, bathroom SO MUCH STUFF TO PACK TOO MUCH Give Jeremy September rent!!! MUST DO THIS How much is the limit on ATM withdrawals, need rent and cyn money for tonight Is work going to be ok? Is this really going to work? Start looking at Elance again when I'm back Find good flight to Rome Did rich book his flight yet? Have to get apartment Domi Nico I hope we get one How am I going to get this blanket and jeans home and my old purse I have to take taxis I have no more money on my Metrocard!! UGH I hope people show up on Friday Will MK be ok with the smoke? I wish we could change it to Under the Volcano Change orders - This fucking change order is still on my desk What about the December change order under my papers Why does it smell like onions in here? Work late today, then see Cyn at 7 Buy packing tape Steal tape gun from work Work til noon tomorrow, go home and pack Call fedex to see what they need on the boxes for customs Get fedex forms from the mail place on Graham Get fedex number from Yira Buy plug adapters Gifts for Vic, Soph, Alex Process check and get euros for Jonty Cancel phone Renew storage insurance Send all addresses to Mom Call loan people Do moving thing at status on Thursday Katie for sushi Thursday, then b&B with Tim and Cal Buy suitcase? Or no? I think no, I'll know after I pack Install AOL on my laptop HSBC Insurance to mom Have Steve look over my computer Accountant! Oh god the acccountant, when am I going to do that, ooooohhhhh Saturday with the boys, hope that goes OK Sunday where are we going, ask Cal about time frame Saturday need to do rest of shopping and Cal buy clothes, jacket (HM, Gap, Club M) Get plan together for Kim How am I calling in to status on Tuesday? Get SIM on Wednesday, why can't I get it on Tuesday? I hope I get my period soon Need to buy more deodorant and hair shit UGH Clean apartment, Sunday and Monday? Wash sheets and towels, kitchen, floor, bathroom SO MUCH STUFF TO PACK TOO MUCH Give Jeremy September rent!!! MUST DO THIS How much is the limit on ATM withdrawals, need rent and cyn money for tonight Is work going to be ok? Is this really going to work? Start looking at Elance again when I'm back Find good flight to Rome Did rich book his flight yet? Have to get apartment Domi Nico I hope we get one How am I going to get this blanket and jeans home and my old purse I have to take taxis I have no more money on my Metrocard!! UGH I hope people show up on Friday Will MK be ok with the smoke? I wish we could change it to Under the Volcano Change orders - This fucking change order is still on my desk What about the December change order under my papers Why does it smell like onions in here?

2005-09-16

Yesterday was a huge productive day in terms of moving logistics - packed all the boxes, met with key people at work, figured out the FedEx forms for foreign shipments, made some phone calls I needed to make. I feel much less stressed now. I feel like I'm coming down the home stretch. I feel giggly. I feel like my life is about to start.

Then the best damn sushi ever with Katie, then met up with Tim and Cal and a ton of Tim's friends at Bar & Books. It was a fun everyone talking at once lots of hugs Lautrec light smoky haze sweet wine night. It will go down as one of my favorites.

It was especially emotional for me, as Katie was the sole witness to my first escape from America. It was she who I called all night when I fled. It was she who harbored me, who hid me away, who comforted me, who made sure I ate (and drank), who dropped everything to help me discard my old life in the grandest style.

And it is she who accepts the new me, my new boyfriend, and my new life; not only accepts it but embraces it and cheers me on and laughs with me and at me and who will always, always be there with her smile, her sofa, her stash of Valium and Veuve and smokes, and her fierce brand of friendship that seems like something between a pact with the devil and winning the lottery.

2005-09-19

I am emotionally, physically, and spiritually spent.

It's time to go.

Chapter Twenty-eight

2005-09-21

Aaaaaaaand we're back.

Smooth flight, but American Airlines has shitty, cramped seats and inedible food. Another airline to cross off my list.

Awesome trainride; slept the whole way.

Everything is right and real.

2005-09-22

Cal took me to a fabulous late night dinner (as we are want to do here in civilization) of moules gratine and veaux anglais and CREME BRULEE with strawberries. Cal had rocking coq au vin and the biggest effing slab of foie gras EVER that was like BUTTAH. I want to go there again and just have the foie and the moules.

The afternoon sunlight on the big street down to the Internet place covers everything in an instantly nostalgic glow. I know this street is called something like St.

Miss Expatria

Guilleme, but for me it is The Big Street Down To The Internet Place.

It has iguanas on it, and a cheesemakers' shop, and a chocolate shop where today I saw an old woman girlishly stop and wonder at the extravagent confections, and the Other Butcher, and a key maker's stand, and there are lush flowers in enormous pots hanging over the street. It's a film set, and all too real, and I live in the South of France.

For now.

Coming home with Cal and even with the absolute horrific shittiness of his miniscule apartment, having it be home, a safe and comfortable place, where we are HOME and together and nothing else matters.

Tiny cars, motorinos, fugues of French accents, British accents, Irish accents, and our own American accents, Camembert and foie and tiny crackly toasts and Cal cooking up some paupiette stew, glasses and plates clinking from the restaurant below, euros in my pocket, Fortuna Blues in my purse, dressing not for work but just to be fetching, feeling beautiful, having Montpel hair, luxury defined not in menu prices or name brands but in the way it makes you feel alive.

The lack of that high hum in my soul, of my soul fighting against everything I encounter. It's quiet now inside of me.

Chapter Twenty-nine

2005-09-27

I am going.

To Rome.

THIS WEEKEND.

My streets, my language, my food, my wine, my boys, my laughter, my sounds, my stores, my life, my sins, my soul.

James Ellroy said it best: *My city. My wonder.*

2005-09-28

My friend MK gave birth to a beautiful son the other day.

It's just a moment for me. She is one of my closest friends, and it is such a huge thing that she has a baby. For all the ways we are so different, she is so much the person I could be in a parallel life. She took one path and I took another, and I think that we both watch each other's lives unfold and never have to wonder about the road not taken.

Miss Expatria

It makes me think about the road I did take, though. Tonight at dinner, Cal and I talked about going to Amsterdam, Barcelona, Rome; all the fun plans we have for our life, together at last.

What place would a baby have in this life? There is a part of me that wants to keep going with this life I love so much. And there is another part of me that wants to get married and raise a child. How to put these two separate lives into one? Is it impossible? Is it probable?

I see Cal sleeping on the couch and I see him being the father of my children; but we are so selfish about the life we live! There would have to come a point where the magic of having a child outweighs the other magic moments that for now make up my life.

I don't know how to plan. I don't know how to think of things long-term. We could have a child - and then what? Adulthood is around the bend and I am not sure if I am ready for it, if he is, if we are finished truly finished exploring the self-centered lives that we have carved out for ourselves.

Epilogue

2005-10-03

Finally, my soul is still.

Almost three years to the day, I am back in Rome and all is right with the world.

I took the train to Nice, and then took a couchette train, with six beds in the room! I was bunked with the best possible people, considering - an old couple from Sapri, a fabulous French lady who reminded me of my Aunt Janet, and a mom and son who were German-looking but were actually Italian - I couldn't place their accents.

We had a long stop in Ventimiglia, the first one over the border in Italy, and I got out and had a cig and chatted with the French lady. Across the platform was a train full of scouts in tidy uniforms, and nurses that looked like from World War II with their exaggerated white caps and aprons. They were all leaning out the windows, yapping with parents and relatives on the platform and laughing and texting on cell phones. It was quite a scene.

Miss Expatria

And then the train started moving and there came a wave of ciao ciao ciao ciao ciao ciao ciao ciaos, and someone was playing a little tune on a recorder, and I knew I was home.

And then the next thing I knew, the conductor was rousing us all with gentle nudges and whispering, "Roma." I went out and stood at the corridor window and watched the sun rise over hills and stone pines and abandoned farms and vineyards and rolling hills and then we went through a tunnel and BAM! There was the back of St. Peter's Basilica. I gasped. What an entrance.

I got off the train and there was Marco running towards me, laughing and waving, and we hugged and laughed and cried. He drove me down via Cavour to the absolutely spectacular sight of early morning bright orange sunlight over the Fori Imperiali; then up the hill to have coffee overlooking the Colosseum, at our special bar.

And the whole time we're talking and laughing and knowing this is where I belong.

Then to Marco and Viola's new place, and more talking, and Marco preparing things for lunch, sneaking me tastes. Then a nap until Giovanni came over, bearing wine and hugs and fabulousness.

Then lunch and Veuve and wine and pastries and card games; Vincenzo came over and more hugging, more chatting and laughing and playing cards and doing our thing; then Viola came home and got ready for a date and was the same Viola - very beautiful and complaining about everything in her funny, sarcastic, self-depricating way.

Then a deep, satisfying sleep.

I awoke to an empty apartment; walked around, looked at my stuff that Marco and Viola have incorporated into their new apartment; smoked on the terrace and watched the trains; was at peace.

As I was getting ready to leave the house, I passed a mirror and did a double take: I finally saw me. I could SEE MYSELF.

I remembered how much I love myself. I remembered what an unstoppable force of nature I am. I remembered how much I love Cal; I love him with a fierceness that aches.

I remembered everything material and emotional that is important to me - as if it was a dream - a dream where you open up the dusty old trunk in the attic and there are all these objects and papers and fabrics from some dreamlike past, and it triggers something profound.

In real life, you wake up from that dream and you have a lingering feeling on the edge of your brain that drifts away as you start your day; but in my life, in this life I have built for myself, it all happened in real time, in full daylight, and I will never, ever let that feeling drift away again.

Breinigsville, PA USA
24 August 2009

PP3733300001B/1/P

9 780615 171463